Learning Capital

The Economic Idea and Causes
of School Quality

Gary Scott

University Press of America, Inc.
Lanham • New York • London

Copyright © 1997 by
University Press of America,® Inc.
4720 Boston Way
Lanham, Maryland 20706

3 Henrietta Street
London, WC2E 8LU England

Library of Congress Cataloging-in-Publication Data

Scott, Gary.
Learning capital : the economic idea and causes of school qualilty /
Gary Scott.
p.   cm.
Includes bibliographical references and index.
1. Education--Economic aspects--United States. 2. Educational
equalization--United States. 3. Academic achievement--United States.
4. Education--United States--Finance. 5. Education and state--United
States.   I. Title.
LC66.S394   1996   379.1'1'0973--dc20   96-34268   CIP

ISBN 0-7618-0489-7 (cloth: alk. ppr.)
ISBN 0-7618-0490-0 (pbk: alk. ppr.)

⊖™The paper used in this publication meets the minimum
requirements of American National Standard for information
Sciences—Permanence of Paper for Printed Library Materials,
ANSI Z39.48—1984

Contents

Tables

Figures

Preface

The relative contributions of a school and a pupil in producing cognitive achievement growth are theoretically isolated so that the efficiency of a school can be evaluated more objectively. Using educational psychology and the neo-classical, economic method of constrained optimization, it is argued that a school is responsible for supplying a pupil with a high learning rate while the pupil's contribution is measured by her time-on-task or attention to a lesson.

Two surprising inferences are drawn from this model of school quality. The most interesting result is that producing equality of achievement outcomes among pupils increases a school's ability to offer a maximum average learning rate given any level of expenditures. This contradicts present theory. A further implication is that the presumed market failure in providing for equality of educational opportunity does not exist since private schools are found to be more equal than state schools. Both of these ideas are empirically supported using the *High School and Beyond* Data. Incorporating these results into an analysis of a voucher policy suggests that efficiency can be increased by 15% and equality of cognitive achievement by 28% without forfeiting any integration within all schools.

Acknowledgments

I have enjoyed the privilege of membership in two scholarly communities during the six years of writing this book. My seminar students and faculty colleagues at Saint Mary's University of Texas have inspired and constructively criticized. My dissertation committee at the University of Notre Dame was prudently skeptical by requiring better clarification of these new ideas concerning the economics of education. Despite the influences of both, an author must assume responsibility for his theories and recommendations, as is done here.

In addition, Dorothy Albritton cheerfully endured Greek Symbols and statistical tables in preparing the final manuscript. The idea that reason alone is sufficient for a good life is repeatedly abandoned with the presence of Lauri. Finally, this book is dedicated to my parents who have made my trips back to Tontogany a homecoming.

Chapter I

The Common School Philosophy

The state finances primary and secondary education through taxation for reasons of efficiency and justice(Benson, 1968; Cohn, 1979; Musgrave, 1989; Levin, 1989, 1991). Allocational efficiency requires at least partial subsidization of education due to the community benefitting from an individual child learning to read, write, calculate, and behave responsibly. Full financing is required so that a child's opportunity to learn is not contingent on family wealth. This full-financing is wise policy.

However, the rationale for the state, rather than the private sector, being the actual provider of primary and secondary education is a distinct and separate issue. The argument is that a state-operated school is the most effective agent in simultaneously attaining the following three common school goals(Mann, 1837; U.S. Supreme Court - Brown v. Board of Education of Topeka, 1954; Tawney, 1961; Dewey, 1966; Coleman, 1966; Rawls, 1971; Mills and Hamilton, 1984; Cremin, 1990; Roemer, 1992; Astin, 1992; Bryk, Lee, and Holland, 1993; Hanushek, 1994):

1) Maximum average cognitive achievement growth per-dollar spent per-pupil.
2) Equality of educational opportunity.
3) Integration of students from different ethnic, racial, socio-economic, and handicap backgrounds.

Common school philosophers believe the typical private school may be superior at attaining the first goal of productive efficiency. But a profit-seeking school could not be trusted to behave in a socially responsible manner with respect to goals two and three. For instance, Horace Mann(1837), the initial author of the common school philosophy, argued that a system of state-provided schools would be "the great equalizer of the conditions of men - the balance wheel of the social machinery.... It does better than to disarm the poor of their hostility towards the rich; it prevents being poor." And with respect to integration, Dewey(1966; pp. 2, 88) argued that the "intermingling in the school of youth of different races, differing religions, and unlike customs create for all a new and broader environment. Common subject matter accustoms all to a unity of outlook...."

These ideas have been persuasive. The United States has committed itself to state-funded as well as state-operated primary and secondary schools. For with the exception of approximately eleven percent of the current student population attending private schools, the United States spent 4.2% of its 1994 GDP in order to enroll 44 million elementary and secondary pupils in these democratically-controlled, public schools. Excluding state and federal administrative expenditures, an average of $6,336 was spent on each pupil.[1]

1.1 The Public School Crisis

Unfortunately, the developmental and equalizing capacity of this system of public education has been criticized by present analysts. Bowles and Gintis(1976, 1988) argue that the equalizing or common school ideal is a myth. They believe "schools are constrained to justify and reproduce inequality rather than correct it."[2]   The constraint is the capitalist mode of production. To preserve social stability, the school must "correspond" to the needs of the economy at large. The need is to reproduce a working and a managerial/capitalist class that does not seriously question the process that determines opportunity. Academic tracking by ability is one policy that accomplishes this task. Finally, they provide persuasive evidence for their conclusion that the system is failing to provide equality of opportunity.

In the 1980's criticism intensified. The focus of alarm was on the system's performance in the development of cognitive abilities for all students, not just the disadvantaged that concerned Bowles and Gintis. This concern was sparked in 1983 when the National Commission on Excellence in Education released its famous report: *A Nation At Risk*. The report was dramatic and urgent in tone:

> Our Nation is at risk. Our once unchallenged preeminence in commerce, industry, science, and technological innovation is being overtaken by competitors throughout the world... the educational foundations of our society are presently being eroded by a rising tide of mediocrity... If an unfriendly foreign power had attempted to impose on America the mediocre educational performance that exists today, we might well have viewed it as an act of war. As it stands, we have allowed this to happen to ourselves.[3]

The eighteen authors of this report who came from higher education, business, and government cited evidence of deteriorating performance. First, in an international comparison of nineteen academic tests, United States students were never first or second and scored last seven times. Second, 13% of all seventeen year olds can be considered functionally illiterate. Finally, the average scores as well as the absolute number of students scoring "high" on standardized college entrance tests have been declining since 1963.[4] Additional critical reports were published during the 1980's.[5] Gloomy predictions were made of social and economic ruin if the rising tide of education mediocrity was not arrested.

Reason for concern has not diminished. Despite increased requirements in math, science, and reading; President Bush's 1991 Council of Economic Advisors wrote that "no performance improvements have been made in these subject areas since the appearance of *A Nation At Risk*."[6] The Clinton Administration concurs that primary and secondary education has deteriorated:

> The United States is squandering one of its most precious resources - the gifts, talents, and high interests of many of its students. In a broad range of intellectual and artistic endeavors, these youngsters are not challenged to do their best work. This problem is especially severe among economically disadvantaged and minority students...[7]

So the public school system as envisioned by Horace Mann in 1837 is suffering a modern-day crisis in developing cognitive abilities and doing it in an equitable fashion.

1.2 Policy Options

So what are the solutions to this crisis? There is no shortage in the number of recommendations. An assumption of most proposals is that the problems can be cured with marginal adjustments within the existing state-controlled system. Examples of these incremental policies include:[8]

1) Increase emphasis on core curriculum subjects such as reading, writing, and math as opposed to music, driver education, and bachelor living.

2) Increase performance expectations by raising graduation requirements and homework assigned.

3) Encourage states to decentralize authority by giving principals and teachers more independence and autonomy.

4) Use of national standardized tests to monitor and encourage cognitive performance.

5) Increase the quality and quantity of instructional materials such as textbooks, media hardware, computers, and laboratory equipment.

6) Expand and improve teacher education and competence, especially in teachers' area of specialty.

7) Increase teacher and principals' salaries in order to attract talent away from private industry. Also, make the salaries market sensitive and performance based.

8) Reduce class sizes so that students can receive more individualized attention.

9) Provide teachers with more time during the school day to prepare their lessons and observe other classes.

10) Improve teacher recruitment methods.

11) Increase funding for research and development of pedagogy and curriculum.

12) Expand special education programs.

Notice that three-fourths (4 through 12) of these proposals involve increased educational expenditures. The remaining proposals(1 through 3) require increased student effort in appropriate subjects and a general desire to decentralize authority.

The alternative to these incremental policies is the voucher plan. Each student would be given a scholarship to be redeemed at the school of the family's choice. The goal is to eliminate the public school monopoly by having schools compete for enrollment and thus revenue. This competition is expected to create incentives for schools to maximize learning with their given budgets. If a school does not perform adequately it would be threatened with decreasing enrollment and decreasing revenue. The idea that competition would be useful to encourage the supply of quality education is well over 200 years old(A. Smith, 1776; Paine, 1792; J.S. Mill, 1859, 1865; Friedman, 1962; Coons and Sugarman, 1978; Chubb and Moe, 1990; Lieberman, 1993). But again, the fear is that equality and integration goals would suffer under a privatized system of education.

To summarize, the performance of Horace Mann's universal, "free," and government operated education system has been found wanting. Available are four policy options to cure the problems. First, increase funding for various programs within the existing public school system. Second, raise the homework and graduation requirements for students within the public system. Third, decentralize authority to achieve flexibility. Or finally, institute competition among schools.

1.3 Can Higher Cognitive Achievement be Purchased?

In order to provide a basis for evaluating these proposed school policies, especially the incremental policies, social scientists use multiple regression models to estimate the educational production function. Once the determinants of high cognitive growth are isolated; policy makers and public-school administrators simply manipulate the policy-oriented, independent variables in pursuit of common school goals one and two.

More specifically, the technical relationship between school resources and cognitive achievement growth must be known in order for a school to be productively efficient as well as equal. Relative input prices are assumed to be given. To maximize mean cognitive achievement within a school, administrators employ inputs that have the highest marginal product per-dollar as their budgets are expanded. Estimating the marginal product of each school input is the goal of production function research or input-output analysis.

When specifying an educational production function, it is important to recognize that schools are not the only source of learning. The non-school factors of family, initial student ability, community, and peer groups must be controlled so that the unique influence of school resources can be isolated. Therefore, the most general production function is expressed as function 1.1.

(1.1) $q = f(v, h, c, p, s)$

where:

$q =$ school output; ideally measured by standardized test score improvement over an instructional time period.

$v =$ vector measuring student ability and motivation prior to formal instruction.

$h =$ vector of family characteristics.

$c =$ vector of community characteristics.

$p =$ vector of academic peer characteristics.

$s =$ vector of school resources.

There have been at least 187 attempts to estimate the educational production function.[9]   Averch, et. al.(1974), Bridge, et. al.(1979) and Hanushek(1986, 1989) provide summaries of this work. Some generalizations can be made from the results of these analyses. Family socio-economic variables and student ability measures have had the largest relative impact on achievement growth during an instructional period. The community and peer effects have been smaller and are frequently ambiguous. Typically, the peer effect is measured by the average of student's pre-test scores, socio-economic status, or proportion minority. The rationale for the peer effect is that the quality of students an individual pupil interacts with exerts an independent influence on the amount learned. Finally, after controlling for student ability, family, community, and peers, the focus can turn to the policy relevant relationship between school resources and student achievement.

The Civil Rights Act of 1964 authorized and funded the classic production-function study, *Equality of Educational Opportunity*(1966), whose principal author was James Coleman. Analyzing the impact of school resources across more than one thousand public schools, his conclusion was disappointing:

> Per-pupil expenditure, books in the library, and a host of other facilities and curricular measures show virtually no relation to achievement if the 'social' environment of the school - the educational backgrounds of other students and teachers - is held constant... family background differences account for much more variation in achievement than do school differences(Coleman; 1966, pp. 71 and 73).

It is discouraging to conclude that the findings have not changed since Coleman's initial study. In fact, no particular school resource has been found to have a consistent and positive effect on academic achievement in all these cross-sectional studies in the past thirty years. Hanushek(1986,1989) has conveniently summarized the results of these accumulated production-function studies which are presented in table 1.1.

Notice the frequency in which the traditional measures of educational quality are either statistically insignificant or significantly negative. Only teacher experience provided any hint of consistency in increasing achievement. But even this measure was statistically insignificant or negative in 71% of the studies. Hanushek commented on the puzzling pattern of school inputs having little impact on achievement:

> Without systematic tabulation of the results of the various studies, it would be easy to conclude that the findings are inconsistent. But there is a consistency: There is no strong or systematic relationship between school expenditures and student performance(Hanushek, 1989; p.47).... If we think of schools as maximizing student achievement, the preceding evidence indicates that schools are economically inefficient, because they pay for attributes that are not systematically related to achievement(Hanushek, 1986; p.1163).

Table 1.1
Estimated Expenditure Parameter Coefficients from 187 Studies of the Educational Production Function for Public Schools from 1956 to Present

Input	Number of studies	Statistically Significant +	-	Total	Statistically Insignificant +	-	unknown sign
Teacher/pupil ratio	152	14	13	125	34	46	45
Teacher education	113	8	5	100	31	32	37
Teacher experience	140	40	10	90	44	31	15
Teacher salary	69	11	4	54	16	14	24
Expenditures/pupil	65	13	3	49	25	13	11
Administrative inputs	61	7	1	53	14	15	24
Facilities	74	7	5	62	17	14	31

Source: Eric Hanushek "The Impact of Differential Expenditures on School Performance," *Educational Researcher*, May 1989, p. 47. For an earlier summary: "The Economics of Schooling: Production and Efficiency in Public Schools," *Journal of Economic Literature*, 1986, 24(3), p. 1163.

Since these studies involved only public schools, a suspicion of inefficiency within the public sector has been established. If cognitive achievement is the primary goal, then it is reasonable to conclude that the incremental policy of increased funding within the present public system is economically irrational. So three-fourths of the incremental policies listed previously would be futile.

After reviewing these studies, Hanushek subscribes to the hypothesis that the lack of competition might explain these poor results:

A suggestion of inefficiency on the part of public schools of course does not come as a great surprise to many for two reasons. First, educational decision makers are apparently not guided by incentives to maximize profits or to conserve on costs. Second, they may not understand the production process and therefore cannot be expected to be on the production frontier. In other words, much of the optimization part of the theory of the firm and competitive markets is questionable in the case of governmental supply in a quasi-monopoly situations....We are prone to accept that without real evidence that for-profit firms are optimizing such that a tabulation of results for competitive firms would look different from table [1.1]. We at least know that for-profit firms that are not maximizing are more likely to go out of existence than a public enterprise not maximizing(Hanushek, 1986; p. 1166).

To conclude, additional funding is not being transformed into higher cognitive achievement on the margin within public schools. This has been interpreted as evidence of productive inefficiency or monopoly behavior. However, efficiency is a relative concept. Are these poor results peculiar to public schools or characteristic of all education, both public and private?

1.4 Do Private Schools Perform Better?

To answer this question, the United States Department of Education conducted the *High School and Beyond* Survey, which resulted in the largest data set ever collected on secondary education.[10]   The most important characteristic of this data set is that it contained test scores and family background measures for students in both the public and private sectors. Since the participation rate of private, non-Catholic schools was too low in the sampling; a comparison could only be made between students in public and Catholic high schools. The method employed was a logical extension of the preceding production-function analysis. The only difference was that a Catholic-school dummy variable was substituted into the regression model in place of school resources. If private-school enrollment significantly shifted cognitive achievement upward for the individual pupil, then perhaps school competition, rather than increased funding, would be the best policy to improve education.

The measured effects of Catholic schooling or competition was positive and statistically significant. However, there remains disagreement about what the positive parameter for the dummy variable really means and whether the size of the Catholic advantage has any practical significance. Coleman, Hoffer, and Greeley(1985) found a Catholic school advantage ranging from 15.4% to 39% depending on the model specification. Coleman and Hoffer(1987) and Coleman(1987) have attributed this advantage to the superior "functional" community surrounding a Catholic school which they call "social capital." The mingling of parents, teachers, students, and administrators within a parish-school encourages higher academic "norms" to be established. Whereas public-school communities are an inferior proxy for the increasingly deficient family in contemporary society. Simply put, public-school students do not interact as much with adult role models that have higher intelligence and display a more disciplined work and study ethic.

Chubb and Moe(1990) also found a private school advantage of similar size using the *High School and Beyond* Data. However, they attributed the advantage to the excessive bureaucratization of public schools which impeded their ability to "develop clear objectives and high academic expectations...(Chubb and Moe, 1990)."

Bryk, Lee, and Holland(1993) offer a third explanation for the private school advantage discovered in the *High School and Beyond* Data: "a constrained academic structure, communal school organization, and an inspirational ideology are the major forces that shape the operation of individual Catholic schools and contribute to their overall effectiveness(p.11)." In other words, the relatively larger proportion of students enrolled in advanced academic courses in Catholic schools accounts for their higher achievement.

Finally, Willms(1985) and Alexander and Pallas(1985) also conducted independent analyses of the data using somewhat different control variables. They also found a positive and statistically significant Catholic advantage; but it was smaller. Alexander and Pallas concluded that the sector difference was "substantively trivial"(1985, p. 115) from a practical perspective. Willms(1985; p. 113) concurred: "policy decisions should not be based on the assumption that either public or private schools produce better achievement outcomes." So there is disagreement as to what causes the private-Catholic advantage and whether there is even a sufficiently large Catholic advantage to bother investigating.

The preceding interpretations of the private advantage need to be evaluated. To begin, it is frustrating to assert that there exists a private advantage without tracing it to a specific policy of the school that differs from the policy of the inferior public schools. For example, Chubb and Moe(1990) found a statistically significant link between public-school bureaucratic constraints and low student test scores. But why should a rigid hierarchy lead to lower academic performance? It may lead to higher costs, but that is not the dependent variable or what is trying to be explained. Cognitive test score growth is the dependent variable. It is difficult to imagine how bureaucratic behavior influences student effort and teaching quality within the typical classroom. Without a specific theory establishing the relationship, the statistical significant relationship could be merely spurious with some unidentified variable that varies across sectors. The crucial question is whether public-school student achievement would increase if the bureaucracies were somehow streamlined. Their theoretical or causal link between political-bureaucratic constraints and classroom learning was vague and unpersuasive. By focusing on the bureacracy and its behavior attention is diverted away from the more technical determinants of high cognitive learning within the typical classroom.

Bryk, Lee, and Holland(1993) do focus on the differential classroom experience between public and Catholic school pupils. Again, they argue that Catholic school pupils achieve more due to being challenged with a more advanced, academic curriculum. As a result, Bryk, Lee, and Holland(1993) implicitly recommend that public schools adopt a more "constrained academic structure." In other words, public schools should imitate Catholic schools by enrolling more pupils in more advanced academic courses such as calculus as opposed to general math.

However, this policy is not as simple as it may seem. In fact, it might stunt the public school pupils' academic progress. Prematurely placing a pupil in an advanced, academic course before mastering prerequisites would cause the public school curriculum to become unintelligible. So imposing a more "constrained academic structure" on public schools could potentially exacerbate the gap between Catholic and public school achievement due to public school pupils becoming overwhelmed.

Finally, the essence of the "social capital"(Coleman and Hoffer,1987; Coleman, 1987) explanation is that public schools are bad because communities and families have disintegrated. This sociological theory is largely independent of technical school policies that can be practically employed even by a school entrepreneur under a voucher system. What starts out as an analysis of school excellence and the effects of competition turns into a criticism of modern society and culture. Should it not be presumed that the education system is or should be the prime mover of the culture and not vice versa? No doubt, there is a simultaneous interaction. But the school should try to disrupt this anti-intellectual cycle since the parents of the present pupils were also educated in the same defective public-school system. Also, it is not clear whether market competition had any role in causing the superior Catholic, intellectual "community." From a policy perspective, this theory has little to offer concerning the question of how to fix the ailing public schools except to merely encourage parents, students, teachers, and administrators to interact and collaborate more.

To their credit however, Coleman, Hoffer, and Greeley(1985) and Coleman and Hoffer(1987) did show that the Catholic sector students took more courses and thus did more corresponding homework which may have caused higher achievement. But why did private-sector students exert more effort? Was it because private school teachers and administrators adopted higher academic standards due to market forces? Or was it because more committed and motivated pupil/families selected themselves into the private sector? Goldberger and Cain(1983) and Rosenbaum and Rubin(1983) raise the latter question by arguing that the family and student-ability information available in the data set may be inadequate in controlling for this selection bias.

In summary, the results of all this educational research has been disappointing. Increased funding has been shown to be largely ineffective in raising cognitive achievement. And the results on competition seem inconclusive. Commenting on the public-private school debate, Alexander and Pallas(1985, p. 116) state: "Neither side has produced the proverbial smoking gun, and neither side seems much impressed with the arguments advanced by the opposition." Perhaps at best, the evidence demonstrates that a voucher policy might help somewhat but would not be a panacea. Finally, increasing homework and graduation requirements is not as simple a policy as it may seem. Just because a teacher assigns more homework does not mean the students actually do it(McKenzie, 1977; Murnane, 1984). So the underlying and more pressing question of how to raise student effort remains unanswered.

In addition to the futility of funding and competition, no great gains are to be enjoyed through the peer variable because it inevitably involves a zero-sum effect. For if mean student-body ability raises an individual student's achievement, then mixing students raises the cognitive growth of students below the mean while lowering it for those above. The only possibility for an overall efficiency gain is for the individual gains of students below the mean to exceed the individual losses of those above the mean. The evidence is ambiguous on this matter(Henderson, Mieszkowski, and Sauvageau, 1978; Arnott and Rowse, 1987; Gyimah-Brempong and Gyapong, 1991). The same zero-sum effect characterizes the mean socio-economic status of student-bodies as well as the proportion of minority students in a school. In conclusion, there is no convincing evidence that any of the preceding policy recommendations would dramatically stimulate intellectual growth in our schools.

1.5 Educational Nihilism

Given this literature review, what is the current state of educational thought? Humility has permeated the educational vision. No longer is it believed that formal school interventions can dramatically alter a pupil's intellectual development. For instance, Summers and Wolfe(1977) state: "Most empirical attempts to identify which inputs matter have concluded that schools barely make a difference. From this conclusion has flowed a prevailing nihilism with respect to schools as an egalitarian force."

So the production-function analyses leads to the conclusion that schools are relatively superfluous in altering the mean level and final distribution of cognitive abilities. The ensuing policy debate frequently involves families blaming the schools and schools blaming the families for intellectual demise. Given this, one might expect confusion and disorder to overtake the scholarly articles appearing in the numerous journals dedicated to studying education. However, this has not been the case.

Despite the finger-pointing in policy debates and discouraging research findings, there still exist three ideas that consistently and persistently appear in the literature concerning the nature of formal schooling. These ideas are distinct but related and are adhered to by most educational analysts and policy makers. The first two ideas are descriptive or positive statements concerning the nature of educational technology. The third idea is a normative or policy-oriented belief stemming from the first two ideas. These three elements that define current educational theory are now outlined.

1) *Pupils can be differentiated by their intellectual capacity to transform educational resources into cognitive growth.*   The first element of current educational thought is that pupils can be distinguished by their natural intellectual abilities. What does this mean? Suppose ten randomly chosen students were each allocated an equal amount of educational resources for the purpose of studying any academic subject. The resources are money and time. The money is used to purchase instruction from a teacher, textbooks, etc. Each pupil can be differentiated by their capacity to transform these resources into intellectual growth.   The more growth during the learning period the higher the ability or aptitude of the pupil. So a pupil's aptitude is synonymous with his rate of learning.   The best proxy measure for this aptitude is present score on a cognitive achievement test that measures general knowledge, reading comprehension, and reasoning skills. So the larger a pupil's present stock of knowledge and reasoning skills the more efficient he learns in future instructional periods.

Few researchers commit to whether aptitude is genetically or environmentally determined.   They usually argue that it is a combination of both. The following references demonstrate that the idea of differential, natural-aptitudes is pervasive:

> Children, as the schools receive them, differ markedly in their docility[teachability] - due in part to innate ability, but perhaps due more to the economic status and cultural practices of their families.
>   - John Roemer "Providing Equal Educational Opportunity:
>   Public Vs. Voucher," *Social Philosophy and Policy*(1992,
>   p. 291)

> we might expect a positive relationship between growth and initial status; that is, we might expect the initially more-able students to grow at a faster rate than the less-able students.
>   - J.D. Willms "Catholic-school Effects on Academic
>   Achievement: New Evidence from the High School and
>   Beyond Follow-up Study," *Sociology of Education* (1985,
>   p. 105)

ipt...

It could be argued that the different, and potentially more advantageous, academic organization of Catholic high schools is nothing more than a selection phenomena - that the organization is possible because more able and academically ambitious students choose to attend Catholic schools...
> - Anthony S. Bryk, Valerie E. Lee, and Peter B. Holland
> *Catholic Schools and the Common Good*(Harvard University Press, 1993) p. 115

All things being equal, students who enter high school with more cognitive aptitude, sharper basic skills, and more academic knowledge should learn more rapidly than students with less of these attributes of student ability... the strongest influence on achievement gains is student ability, as measured by initial student achievement. If a student could have his academic ability raised from the bottom to the top quartile, and have all else remain exactly the same, that student's gain in achievement over the final two years of high school would increase by .65 year. That is plainly a substantial amount.
> -J.E. Chubb and T. M. Moe *Politics, Markets, and America's Schools*(The Brookings Institute; 1990, pp. 116, 128, and 129)

Altogether, the sources of inequality of educational opportunity appear to lie first in the home itself and the cultural influences immediately surrounding the home; then they lie in the schools' ineffectiveness to free achievement from the impact of the home, and in the school's cultural homogeneity which perpetuates the social influences of the home and its environs.
> - James Coleman *The Public Interest*(1966, pp. 73 and 74)

Research confirms that the higher a student's aptitude or intelligence, the greater the learning in economics. The pretest score is typically the single most important variable in explaining attainment.
> - William Becker, William Greene, and Sherwin Rosen
> "Research on High School Economic Education,"
> *American Economic Reveiew - Papers and Proceedings*(May, 1990; p. 16)

describing the "veil of ignorance" contained in his theory of justice: "nor does any one know his fortune in the distribution of natural assets and abilities, his intelligence, strength, and the like."
> - John Rawls *A Theory of Justice*(1971) p. 12

The efficient allocation of scarce educational resources requires the identification of different individuals' abilities...(1975, p. 292). The quantity of education obtained by an individual conveys information because it is more costly for a less able individual to acquire education than for a more able individual(1987, p. 30).

> - Joseph Stiglitz "The Theory of 'Screening,' Education, and the Distribution of Income," *American Economic Review*(1975) and "The Causes and Consequences of the Dependence of Quality on Price," *Journal of Economic Literature*(March, 1987)

the student's I.Q. or SAT score represents the student's ability to translate time into increased knowledge... Brighter students need apply less effort[time] to achieve the same gain in wealth[achievement] as do less bright students.

> - James N. Wetzel "Measuring Student Scholastic Effort: An Economic Theory of Learning Approach," *Journal of Economic Education*(1977)

The systematic individual component represents differences in intelligence, motivation, unmeasured family inputs, and other things that directly contribute to performance - factors often labeled simply as individual 'ability.'

> - Eric A. Hanushek and Lori L. Taylor "Alternative Assessments of the Performance of School: Measurements of State Variations in Achievement," in *Journal of Human Resources*(Spring 1990) p. 181

Abler persons are more likely to receive public and private scholarships, and thus have their supply curves shifted downward. Or children from higher-income families probably, on the average, are more intelligent and receive greater psychic benefits from human capital.

> - Gary S. Becker *Human Capital*(1975) pp. 116-117

Assumption number two of their educational production model: "A student has only one relevant attribute prior to schooling, innate ability..."

> - Richard Arnott and John Rowse "Peer Group Effects and Educational Attainment," *Journal of Public Economics*(1987) p. 289

Some abilities may be inherited: Within every family there are clear differences in physical and mental abilities. And the theory of genetics teaches us that there will be even more dispersion in abilities across families.
> - Paul A. Samuelson and William D. Nordhaus *Economics*(1985, 12th edition) p. 747

Intelligence is a very general mental capability that, among other things, involves the ability to reason, plan, solve problems, think abstractly, comprehend complex ideas, *learn quickly* . . . (italics added)
> - signed statement by 52 experts in intelligence and allied fields, *Wall Street Journal* (December 13, 1994; editorial page).

So pupils can be differentiated by their intellectual capacities to benefit from educational resources no matter whether it was of physiological or cultural origin. In some of the research this idea is empirically discovered, for the regression parameter for pre-test scores has been positive and statistically significant. In the more theoretical analyses, the idea of naturally "bright" and naturally "dense" students often appears as a working assumption(McKenzie and Staaf, 1976).

2) *A tradeoff exists between equality and efficiency in the production of cognitive achievement.* The second element of educational dogma follows directly from the first. If students can be differentiated by aptitude or learning rate, then it necessarily follows that there exists a tradeoff between efficiency and equality. Taking one dollar and one hour of study from a low-aptitude student and re-allocating it to a high-aptitude student raises the average cognitive growth between the two students. For the high-aptitude pupil's gain is quite large compared to the lower-aptitude pupil's loss. As a result, average achievement can be raised at the expense of equality in the context of a fixed educational budget. This inequality appears along both aptitude and family-income lines since aptitude is positively correlated to family socio-economic status. This tradeoff has been articulated by social scientists with divergent methodological and political philosophies:

Indeed, if by greater ability we mean in part the ability to learn more easily, then it is more efficient(if our objective is maximizing net national output) to spend more resources on the more able... There is some social return to this, since the amount of education which is optimal for the less able is less than that which is optimal for the more able... The efficiency losses in attempting to train a moron to be an engineer are obvious... There is thus the possibility that in imparting more skills to the abler students, we will simultaneously increase the inequality of income.
> - Joseph Stiglitz "The Theory of 'Screening,' Education, and the Distribution of Income," *American Economic Review*(1975, pp. 294, 298)

Writing in the *Columbia University Forum* in 1961 sociologist Seymour Martin Lipset noted that American society had evolved in such a way as to bring into prominence two basic values "which are not entirely compatible and never have been(Lipset, 1961; p.17)." These were Equality and Achievement.
> - Willis Rudy(Professor of History) *Schools in an Age of Mass Culture*(1965, p. 143)

Producing equality of outcomes rather than mere equality of opportunity "would either be terribly costly, or would involve not educating 'bright' children as much as they should be for society's sake, as well as for their own."
> - John Roemer "Providing Equal Educational Opportunity: Public Vs. Voucher," *Social Philosophy and Policy*(1992, p. 292)

Efficiency has not been a top priority issue of school finance reform. Efficiency could entail a trade off involving calculating equity gains versus the costs in efficiency terms of the reform.
> - Allan Odden "State and Federal Pressures for Equity and Efficiency in Education Financing," in *Financing Education: Overcoming Inefficiency and Inequity*(1982, p. 312), eds. Walter W. McMahon and Terry G. Geske

resources for education are not to be allotted solely or necessarily mainly according to their return as estimated in productive trained abilities, but also according to their worth in enriching the personal and social life of citizens, including here the less favored.
> - John Rawls *A Theory of Justice*(1971), p. 107

In discussions it has been argued that even if selecting students of ability and allocating large amounts of resources to them did in fact maximize national income and the growth rate, one should move toward equalizing expenditures per pupil because it would lead to a more desirable distribution of economic and cultural benefits.

> - George E. Johnson and Frank P. Stafford "Social Returns to Quantity and Quality of Schooling," in *The Journal of Human Resources*, VIII(2), Spring 1973, p. 152.

Even severe critics of the distribution of incomes have generally protested only against unequal opportunities, and have treated inequality resulting from differences in ability with indulgence, if not positive affirmation. Possibly this simply reflects a basic philosophical distinction; I suspect, however, that partly reflected also is an implicit judgment about the interaction between equality and efficiency... The elasticities of and differences among demand curves... are less related to man-made factors, and more to the embodiment of capital in human beings, differences in intelligence, and other basic forces that are less easily corrected.

> - Gary S. Becker *Human Capital*(1975), pp. 129-130

Poorer families have a conflict between equity and efficiency and invest more in abler children only if efficiency outweighs equity... The conflict between efficiency and equity is reduced when abler children are altruistic and are concerned about the welfare of their siblings... Poorer families then could also gain the efficiency of investing more human capital in abler children without sacrificing the interests of other children, for the abler would voluntarily transfer resources to the others when they became adults. In poorer families the amount invested in human capital directly depends on the abilities(as well as the number) of siblings, because poorer parents must choose between the equity and the efficiency of their investments.

> - Gary S. Becker *A Treatise on the Family*(1991) pp. 190-191

One may, in fact, conjecture that it is a misplaced emphasis on equality in education that is responsible for policies in American Education that have led to students' poor performance. The emphasis on equality means that the focus in education is on the bottom of the performance distribution. My general conjecture is this: Policies that focus on high levels of achievement and rewards for high levels reverberate downward through the system, providing an incentive

for students at lower levels to improve(p. 261).... . The data, taken
from the first IEA study(conducted in 1970-71), show that in science,
high achievement growth between ages 10 and 14 is associated with
high variation among students in science achievement. The
presumption is that the same policies that produce high variation in
achievement(presumably selection on merit) also produce higher
mean achievement(footnote, p. 261).
     - James S. Coleman "Some Points on Choice in Education,"
     Sociology of Education, October 1992, pp. 260-262.

In summary, the natural-aptitude belief leads to the equality-
efficiency tradeoff whether articulated explicitly by an author or not.
So schools and teachers are not completely irrelevant or superfluous.
They are more skill-identifiers and resource allocators than they are
skill developers.   The intra-school and inter-school allocation of
resources has important implications for the mean achievement level
as well as the distribution of cognitive abilities at the end of formal
schooling. This may seem inconsistent with the preceding evidence
on the effect of funding(Hanushek, 1986, 1989).   However, the
production-function work wasn't sensitive to the co-determinous effect
of combining funding with ability. In other words, the marginal impact
of funding within public schools could be low due to concentrating a
disproportionate amount of resources on lower-aptitude students in
order to provide equality of opportunity(Brown and Saks, 1975;
Coleman, 1992; Stiglitz, 1993).   So the idea that more equality of
opportunity involves less mean achievement growth with a fixed
educational budget is the second element of current thought.

    3) *Since profit-seeking schools would sacrifice too much equality
of opportunity in favor of efficiency, it is necessary to have state-
controlled, public schools.*   The final idea follows from the equality-
efficiency tradeoff. If the average cognitive growth within a particular
school can increase with unequal allocation of resources among
students, then the market fails to provide for the common good. In
other words, the production of education involves placing social
welfare weights or prices on students. The higher the weight or price
the more a teacher's attention or school's budget is allocated toward
that student. The weights applied to low-income, low-aptitude pupils
in private schools would be excessively low since the rate-of-return

in cognitive growth from this allocation would be lower. Hence, the typical proprietary school would produce a sub-optimal amount of distributive justice by its unfair allocation of educational resources and thus educational opportunity.

Therefore, economic logic leads us full circle back to Horace Mann's original vision of the state controlled, common school. It would solve the market failure. Market-based or private schools would weight lower-aptitude students too low and thus would be inequitable and unfair. On the other hand, the public school would be the "great equalizer of the conditions of men." The common school system would mitigate the unequal forces already rampant in the general economy such as the family transmission of wealth, privilege, and intellectual ability. So democratically-controlled, state schools are necessary both to integrate and insure more equality of opportunity relative to profit-seeking schools:

> There is thus the possibility that in imparting more skills to the abler students, we will simultaneously increase the inequality of income. This has made the organization of the educational system, and the method by which the levels of screening and skill acquisition are determined, an intensely political question.
> - Joseph Stiglitz "The Theory of 'Screening,' Education, and the Distribution of Income," *American Economic Review*(1975, p. 294)

> One of the educational system's great strengths - its commitment to egalitarian education - may impair one of its basic objectives, to provide the most able students with the skills required to help the country sustain technological superiority. An increasing commitment to egalitarianism means that a larger proportion of the available resources go into raising slower learners up to a minimal level than in helping faster learners cover as much material as they can.
> - Joseph Stiglitz *Economics*(1993, p. 1013)

> the public school is egalitarian it two ways: it accepts all students, and it need not 'price-discriminate' among child types... . There are two virtues of a public school system over a voucher system with add-ons: what may be a necessary condition for equal educational opportunity is fulfilled... and constrained Pareto-efficiency is achieved without the necessity of differential tuitions

according to child-type... . Therefore, the public school is an institution which solves the market failure afflicting any voucher or private system... real vouchers will not place the 'right' prices on children.

> - John Roemer   "Providing Equal Educational Opportunity:
> Public Vs. Voucher," *Social Philosophy and Policy*, 1992,
> pp. 307-309

Finally, it is important to face up to the issue of delineating explicitly our normative criteria on what 'should' be the distribution of outputs. We must place 'values' on the outputs... This discussion has assumed implicitly that it is students' valuations that should count. There are many who feel, however, that valuations should be made by other groups, such as the faculty, the college administration, the taxpayers, or particular groups of students.

> - W. Lee Hansen, Allen C. Kelley and Burton A. Weisbrod
> "Economic Efficiency and the Distribution of Benefits
> from College Instruction," *American Economic
> Review*(1970)

Popular arguments for a system of market controls in education commonly employ a microeconomic explanation that bears little relation to the ideas about schools-as-communities... Under this microeconomic view, teachers' entrepreneurial motives would make schools into more efficient service providers. This conception of teacher thinking and behavior is quite antithetical, however, to the social foundations of a communal school organization... These observations are relevant in part because so much of the current rhetoric about privatization and choice can be traced to studies by Coleman and others on public and private schools... For example, the more equitable social distribution of achievement... that occurs in Catholic schools does not typify other private schools(p. 311)... These findings raise doubts about any blanket statement that a move toward greater privatization will ensure better consequences for students(p. 312)... Market forces cannot explain the broadly shared institutional purpose of advancing social equity... Likewise, market forces cannot easily explain why resources are allocated within schools in a compensatory fashion in order to provide an academic education for every student(p. 300).

> - Anthony S. Bryk, Valerie E. Lee, and Peter B. Holland
> *Catholic Schools and the Common Good*

The rationale for the public provision of education seems to be more philosophical and constitutional than economic[i.e. rivalness and excludability]. It derives from notions of equality as expressed in the Declaration of Independence and the U.S. Constitution. More explicitly, most state constitutions require their subdivisions to operate "thoroughgoing and equal" primary and secondary education systems. The purpose is that whatever else *equality* might mean in the constitutional sense, it surely means at least some approximation of equal access to the basic skills needed for functioning in the adult world. If education were left to an unregulated private sector, the quality of education surely would vary significantly according to both the income and tastes of parents.
- Edwin S. Mills and Bruce W. Hamilton *Urban Economics*(1984, 3rd edition) p. 284

The only institution of a free society which serves everyone equally and is controlled by everyone is the government. So the government should control the common schools.
- R. Freeman Butts(prominent educational historian) in John E. Sturm and John E. Palmer eds., *Democratic Legacy in Transition*(1971)

In conclusion, there is a compatibility and coherence between economic thought and the common school philosophy. The two independent schools of thought converge on the preceding three ideas concerning the nature of educational production and the necessary policy stemming from our democratic commitment to equality of opportunity. As a shorthand expression, this general theory containing the preceding three elements is now referred to as the orthodox economic theory of learning.

1.6 Thesis Statement

The purpose of the present work is to argue contrary to all three elements of the orthodox economic theory of learning. In other words, both the theory used to make formal learning intelligible and the corresponding primary and secondary educational policy are flawed. Specifically, it is argued that a distinction must be made between aptitude and a student's rate of learning. Once this distinction is made, it becomes evident that with the exception of the few handicapped pupils, students are more equal than unequal in their natural learning rates when provided with optimal learning conditions. Also, there is no tradeoff between equality of opportunity and efficiency. Even more strongly, it is theoretically argued and empirically demonstrated that equality of outcomes, as opposed to mere equality of opportunity, causes higher efficiency within the typical school. Finally, since a necessary ingredient for maximizing mean cognitive achievement growth per-dollar within a school is the production of equality, the theory of market competition leads us to expect that private schools would produce more equality than public schools. This expectation is borne out at high levels of statistical significance using the largest and most detailed data set ever collected on secondary education.

In other words, the school sectors are ranked as follows with respect to their simultaneous attainment of the three common school goals outlined previously: 1)Catholic 2)private, non-Catholic 3)public. So with respect to the weighting of students with different aptitudes, it is shown that private schools weight lower-aptitude students higher than public schools. Hence, there is a state or government failure, not a market failure, in providing for equality of opportunity.

No doubt, this thesis is quite counter-intuitive given the prevailing orthodox economic theory of learning. However, these conclusions are reached without introducing any radical nor even novel theory of learning. The intellectual roots of this argument can be traced to the seminal work of John Carroll(1963) and Benjamin Bloom(1974, 1976). Their work has been omitted from the theoretical specification of production functions as well as the corresponding interpretation of results.[11] One possible reason for their omission is that the theories focus on the management of classroom learning and not school-level or school-system management. But with a few adjustments of their models, rich implications can be derived for an effective educational policy at the school, state, and national levels.

From Carroll's and Bloom's unique perspective, it is argued that the production-function or black-box approach to understanding education is too static or a-historical to account for the forces causing school efficiency over time. In addition, it is demonstrated that the black-box approach, as traditionally specified, has been insensitive in measuring the most important characteristic of a school - the quality of the teacher-pupil interaction. For example, is the curriculum as presented by teachers in their lectures and textbooks too sophisticated and overwhelming for the typical pupil and thus causing confusion? Or alternatively, is the curriculum too elementary or redundant for students' current state of intellectual development and thus causing boredom and idleness? If either of these are the case, little intellectual growth will occur and the standard production-function empirical model will convey the idea that resources don't matter when in fact they do but under more restrictive conditions. These general and vague assertions are defined and defended in detail in subsequent chapters.

To make some general comments in defense of this thesis, Carroll's *Model of School Learning*(1963) is considered the classic in educational psychology. From 1969 to the present, it has consistently appeared over 300 times in the Social Sciences Citation Index. Carroll(1963, p. 73) concluded his path-breaking work by stating that "this conceptual model probably contains, at least at a superordinate level, every element required to account for an individual's success or failure in school learning..." Carroll's research colleagues agreed with his assessment of his own model: "It would appear that in a 20-year history we have little reason to question Carroll's conclusion...(Fisher and Berliner,1985)" that his model contains every element to account for success or failure. Hence, Carroll's model has withstood the test of time.

Bloom's work at the University of Chicago has been both a theoretical refinement and empirical corroboration of Carroll's model. Bloom and his colleagues' work is commonly referred to as *Mastery Learning* and is best summarized in *Human Characteristics and School Learning*(1976). One positive characteristic of their model of learning is that they are much less presuming about a pupil's natural abilities compared to the orthodox economic theory of learning. As evident, both Carroll's and Bloom's work is relatively dated; but let us not subscribe to the fallacy that an old theory is necessarily an obsolete theory. Also, the only weakness of their work is the omission of the concepts of opportunity costs and competing ends. The purpose of the theoretical chapters of this work is to integrate their findings on the nature of group learning with the neo-classical, economic method of constrained optimization.

The outcome of this integrative, theoretical work is a "trickle-up" economic theory of learning. The assumed goal of the school is to maximize mean cognitive achievement growth per-dollar spent among all students within a school. One of two techniques to accomplish this goal is to allocate a disproportionate amount of resources toward the lower-aptitude students at the beginning of any instructional period no matter whether the time period be a day or a year. This eventually benefits all students, both low and high-aptitude. Private schools are expected and in fact do behave in this manner since it is the only way a school can be efficient. This integrated model is believed to be both theoretically reasonable as well as empirically corroborated at high levels of statistical significance.

The final recommendation is that a voucher policy, as specifically defined here, should be adopted because it would: 1) increase mean cognitive achievement growth within all schools in the United States; and 2) increase both within-school and between-school equality of achievement opportunity and equality of achievement outcomes for the entire United States. Due to these dual educational benefits and the intervening formation of human capital, it is further concluded that a policy of school competition is a potent instrument in increasing the growth rate of GDP per labor-hour and minimizing the incidence of poverty partially caused by functional illiteracy.[12]   Finally, all these benefits can be realized at no financial or integration cost.

1.7 Articles of Peace

Questions of educational excellence create passionate argument that frequently turns into useless quarreling. In order to keep the debate focused and prevent premature dismissal of the present thesis, the following comments are offered as gestures for civilized discourse:

A) Educational employees are suspicious of economists and their method that has demonstrated a zero-impact of funding. It is feared that from these results an underlying desire of economists is to contract the overall educational budget and re-allocate the resources to alternative uses. Aggregate budget contraction is not recommended here. The opposite is recommended.

B) It is argued that private provision of education is more efficient and equitable relative to public provision. Given this, it does not necessarily follow that a laissez-faire policy causes more efficiency and more distributive justice in all industries or in all countries or at all times.

C) It is concluded that Catholic schools were superior to private, non-Catholic schools during the sampling period from 1980 to 1982. Some of these private, non-Catholic schools are sponsored by Protestant Churches. From this it does not necessarily follow that the Catholic Religious Tradition is superior to Protestant Religious Traditions.

D) It is neither concluded nor implied that the private school advantage is due to public school administrators and teachers being lazy or incompetent relative to their private school counterparts.

E) It is neither concluded nor implied that the private school efficiency advantage is due to the higher teacher unionization rate within the public sector.

F) The Catholic advantage as argued here does not stem from members of religious orders offering their labor for subsistence wages. Nor is it concluded that it is due to the salary gap among lay teachers. These do make Catholic education cheaper. However, this salary differential and rate of voluntarism is controlled in the regression model and are not used to demonstrate the private advantage.

G) The private school advantage does not stem from the more talented and motivated students selecting themselves into the private sector. It is believed that adequate proxy variables for talent, motivation, and family support are used to control for this acknowledged selection bias. In addition, the private advantage is traced to specific school policies that are independent of pupil quality.

Now that it is better understood what is not being concluded, the argument can begin as to what specific school policies do lead to the private advantage. To understand this argument, a theory of *learning capital* is first developed. Using this theory, it will ultimately be concluded that private schools are superior at minimizing a concept known as *instructional error* in a least-cost manner.

Notes

1 National Center For Education Statistics; U.S. Department of Education, *Digest of Education Statistics*(1995) pp. 11, 34, and 163.

2 Samuel Bowles and Herbert Gintis, *Schooling in Capitalist America: Educational Reform and the Contradictions of Economic Life* (1976, p. 102). Katz(1968), Jencks(1972), and Carnoy and Levin(1976) have argued similarly. These models have provided the foundation for much of the sociological research on primary and secondary education. This is especially the case for the causes and effects of ability tracking within schools. Mehan(1992) provides a summary/critique of this work.

3 National Commission on Excellence in Education, *A Nation At Risk: The Imperative for Educational Reform, 1983.*

4 National Commission on Excellence in Education(1983).

5 Similar reports critical of primary and secondary education include: *Academic Preparation for College: What Students Need to Know and Be Able to Do*, Educational Equality Project, The College Board(1983); *Action for Excellence: A Comprehensive Plan to Improve Our Nation's Schools*, Task Force on Education for Economic Growth, Education Commission of the States(1983); *America's Competitive Challenge: The Need For A National Response*, A Report to the President of The United States from the Business-Higher Education Forum(1983); *High School: A Report on Secondary Education in America*, Ernest Boyer, The Carnegie Foundation for the Advancement of Teaching(1983); *Making the Grade*, Report of the Twentieth Century Fund Task Force on Federal Elementary and Secondary Education Policy(1983); *The Paideia Proposal: An Educational Manifesto*, Mortimer J. Adler on behalf of the members of the Paideia Group(1982); *A Place Called School: Prospects for the Future*, John I. Goodlad(1983); *A Study of High Schools*, Cosponsored by the National Association of Secondary School Principals and the National Association of Independent Schools(1984).

6 Council of Economic Advisors, *Economic Report of the President*, February 1991, p.123.

7 U.S. Department of Education; Office of Educational Research and Improvement, *National Excellence: A Case for Developing America's Talent*(October, 1993) p. 1.

8 See Beatrice Gross and Ronald Gross(eds.) *The Great School Debate: Which Way For American Education?*(1985), Joseph Murphy(ed.) *The Educational Reform Movement of the 1980's: Perspectives and Cases*(1990), and Lawrence Cremin *Popular Education and Its Discontents*(1990).

9 The following is a sampling of the production function work: Mollenkopf and Melville(1956), Benson(1965), Coleman, et. al.(1966), Burkhead,

Learning Capital

Fox, and Holland(1967), Raymond(1968), Bartell(1969), Hanushek(1968, 1970), Bowles(1969), Fox(1969), Michelson(1970), Kiesling(1970), Levin(1970), Katzman(1971), Brown(1972), Averch and Kiesling(1972), Smith(1972), Perl(1973), New York State Education Department(1972, 1974, 1975), Winkler(1975), Bidwell and Kasarda(1975), Murnane(1975), Summers and Wolfe(1977), Brown and Saks(1975), Henderson, Mieszkowski, and Sauvageau(1978), Sebold and Dato(1981), Murnane and Maynard(1981), Glasman and Biniaminov(1981), Chizman and Zak(1983), Heyneman and Loxley(1983), Lee and Bryk(1989), Lopez(1990), Lillydahl(1990), Chubb and Moe(1990), Gyimah-Brempong and Gyapong(1991), Bryk, Lee, and Holland(1993).

10 *High School and Beyond.* Chicago: National Opinion Research Center, 1980.

11 Henry M. Levin has been one of the few economists who has taken notice of Carroll's and Bloom's work. For his interpretation see "The Economic Implications of Mastery Learning" by Levin in *The Limits of Educational Reform* by Martin Carnoy and Henry M. Levin(eds.),1976.

12 George A. Miller "The Challenge of Universal Literacy," *Science,* September 1988, 241, pp. 1293-1299

Chapter II

Tutorial Model of Education

A new economic model of educational production that integrates Carroll's and Bloom's work is necessary in order to define school efficiency and equality precisely. Good instruction and pupil effort are both necessary but neither are sufficient in producing cognitive growth. The goal of this tutorial model is to isolate theoretically the relative contributions of the school and the pupil in producing achievement. This simple model is then complicated in the next chapter in order to demonstrate how equality causes efficiency. In the statistical model it is shown how private schools best exploit this positive relationship between equality and efficiency.

Several simplifying assumptions are made. First, every family has one child-pupil. Second, each family hires an administrator to manage the child's tutorial. Third, the content of the course of study is exogenous. All that is necessary is for achievement growth to be measurable with standardized tests. Finally, the opportunity costs of education are family expenditures and student study time.

2.1 Production Function

According to Carroll(1963) learning is "going from ignorance of some specified fact or concept to knowledge or understanding of it, or of proceeding from incapability of performing some specified act to capability of performing it..." So learning is an incremental addition to a student's present stock of knowledge and skills. To be more technically precise, the educational production function for an individual student is defined and altered as:

(2.1) $A = a + KT$

(2.2) $q = KT$ where: $q = A - a$

(2.3) $K = \dfrac{q}{T}$

(2.4) $K = g(T)$ where: $g' < 0$ for all T

where:

A = student's achievement level at the end of an instructional period as measured by score on a post-test.

a = student's achievement level at beginning of instructional period as measured by a pre-test.

T = total time-on-task both inside and outside the classroom. This is not elapsed time, but rather time concentrating on a lesson.

K = q/T = average rate of learning throughout instructional period. It is a negative function of T due to diminishing returns to T caused by mental fatigue(i.e. $g' < 0$).

q = $A - a$ = learning or cognitive achievement growth as measured by improvement score.

Equation 2.2 can be used to analyze the output in one or several courses. To analyze the output of several courses simultaneously, q is interpreted as the improvement score on a composite test comprised of several sections pertaining to the different subjects.[1] For simplification, it is assumed that there are diminishing returns to time-on-task for all values of T as defined in function 2.4. Given all this, the marginal properties of equation 2.2 are:

(2.5) $\dfrac{\partial q}{\partial K} = T > 0$

$$(2.6) \quad \frac{\partial q}{\partial T} = g'T + K > 0 \quad \text{where: } g' = \frac{\partial K}{\partial T} < 0 \text{ for all } T$$

$$(2.7) \quad \frac{dK}{dT} = \frac{\dfrac{\partial q}{\partial T}}{\dfrac{\partial q}{\partial K}} = \frac{g'T + K}{T} = g' + \frac{K}{T} < 0 \text{ assuming } dq = 0$$

Time-on-task(T) has a clear interpretation. It is the amount of time a student's attention is focused on a lesson. Notice that cognitive growth is zero unless the pupil contributes some attention(T > 0). Again, in the orthodox economic theory of learning the average rate of learning(K) is interpreted as the aptitude of the student. In other words, the higher the aptitude or ability of the student, the more efficient the student transforms time-on-task into achievement growth. The operational measure for this is a score on a general aptitude test such as a college entrance exam. No attention is given to how the school or teacher influences the learning outcome using this interpretation.

Carroll(1963) and Bloom(1974,1976) interpret the average rate of learning differently. They argue that K is the educator's dependent variable. The educator's goal is to maximize K. The aptitude of the student is important; but it merely determines the optimal instructional method employed in the process of maximizing K. Thus, K measures the quality of the school, not the ability of the student. Their interpretation is used here and is crucial for the central thesis.

2.2 Market Exchange in the Tutorial Model

Given Carroll's and Bloom's interpretation, the family influences achievement growth in a direct and indirect manner. First, the pupil, under family guidance, chooses consciously or by default the level of time-on-task(T) throughout the instructional period. Second, the family gives e dollars per-instructional period to the administrator for the purpose of maximizing K. Note that maximizing the average rate of learning is synonymous with maximizing the marginal rate of learning due to the marginal assumptions(see equations 2.3 and 2.6). The administrator's problem can be viewed in the traditional constrained maximization framework:

objective function to be maximized:
(2.8) $K(x_1, x_2, x_3, \ldots x_m)$

budget constraint:
(2.6) $e = p_1 x_1 + p_2 x_2 + p_3 x_3 + \ldots p_m x_m$

Lagrange expression:

(2.7) $L = K(x_1, x_2, x_3, \ldots x_m) - \lambda(e - p_1 x_1 - p_2 x_2 - p_3 x_3 - \ldots p_m x_m)$

where:

K = average rate of learning for the individual pupil
x_j = educational input; $j = 1, 2, \ldots m$
p_j = price of jth educational input; $j = 1, 2, \ldots m$
e = family expenditures or administrator's budget
λ = Lagrangian multiplier

Essentially, the school is to maximize one(K) of the two inputs(K, T) in the pupil-family's production function(2.2) in exchange for e.

The most important role of the administrator when maximizing K is the hiring of the tutor(s). They should be academically competent as well as skillful in adjusting their instruction to fit the student's aptitude. The selection of appropriate textbooks is also important. The primary value of a tutorial is that the instructional sophistication can be custom tailored to the pupil's unique aptitudes. The existence of peers might reduce K by making the instruction either too difficult or redundant.

2.3 *Evaluating the School*

Given that a family commits T and e to a school in exchange for K, the relative efficiency of three schools is illustrated in figure 1.1. School Z, associated with function Z, is superior to G which in turn is superior to M. With an equal amount of time(j) and expenditures(e) allocated to each of the three schools, Z produces the largest growth(q). Or identically, Z produces the largest average rate of learning(K) measured in the graph by the slope xj/0j.

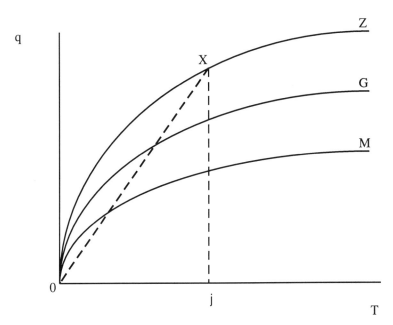

Figure 1.1
Three Educational Production Functions
Corresponding to Three Different Schools

Mathematically, the efficiency of the tutorial is expressed as c in equation 2.12. c is the average cost per-unit of output or the cost-effective ratio for the school. It measures the average performance of a school in transforming funding into a learning rate. School Z, associated with function Z in figure 1.1, offers the lowest value for c among the three schools. The c-ratio is expected to increase with partial increases in expenditures(e) and time(T) due to diminishing returns to expenditures and time. The average rate of learning(K) produced by the school is now referred to as *learning capital*.[2] So learning capital is positively related to the family budget(e) and negatively related to the cost per-unit of learning capital(c) as evident in equation 2.13.

$$(2.12) \qquad c = \frac{e}{K} = \frac{e}{\dfrac{q}{T}} = \frac{eT}{q}$$

$$(2.13) \qquad K = \frac{e}{c}$$

In summary, this tutorial model was used to introduce three important concepts: time-on-task(T), learning capital($K = q/T$), and school efficiency(c). Most important, the relative contributions of the school and the pupil/family in the production of cognitive achievement growth were theoretically isolated. Specifically, the school's contribution to a pupil's intellectual development is measured by c. The lower the value of c, the better is the school. The pupil/family's contribution is measured directly by T and indirectly by e. This simple model is complicated in the next chapter in order to account for the dynamics of group learning in a classroom setting.

Notes

1   McKenzie and Staaf(1974) describe how the average rate of learning(K) and time-on-task(T) are then interpreted as a weighted average for their respective values in each course.

2   Learning capital, rate of learning, and learning rate will be used as synonymous terms for K.

Chapter III

Classroom Model of Education

There is a benefit and a cost associated with group instruction compared to the tutorial. The benefit is that teacher costs, which comprise most of educational expenditures(approximately 80%), can be shared by the families of the pupils within a common classroom. However, an inevitable conflict arises if students differ in their current achievement or aptitude levels. Increasing the sophistication of the curriculum may increase the learning rate for high-aptitude students while lowering it for low-aptitude students. Thus, each pupil/family may pay the same expenditure but enjoy different learning rates. So a significant omission of the orthodox economic theory of learning is the impact that the sophistication of the curriculum has on a pupil's rate of learning. The preceding benefit and cost of classroom learning are now analyzed in detail. The analysis in this chapter results in a more general mathematical model of learning and school quality that builds upon the tutorial model.

3.1 The Theory of Instructional Error

To understand the potential conflict between pupils within a single classroom, Bloom(1976) defines *instructional error* as the extent to which the sophistication of a course is inappropriate for a student's present ability. The course can be either too elementary and thus redundant, just right, or too difficult and thus overwhelming. For example, if a student has mastered differential calculus, the student's learning rate under a basic algebra curriculum would be close to zero. A student with a weak vocabulary and low familiarity with basic sentence structure would have a near-zero learning rate in a course on Shakespeare. So the rate of learning decreases in proportion to the level of instructional error the ith student experiences. To formally introduce this into the model, let the ith student's aptitude be defined by 3.1:

$$(3.1) \quad V_i = (S_{1i}, S_{2i}, S_{3i}, \ldots S_{ji})$$

V_i = ith pupil's aptitude vector   i = 1,2,3, ...N
S_{ji} = ith pupil's percentage score on the jth aptitude test
        j = 1,2,3, ...m   i = 1,2,3, ...N

These aptitude tests typically measure a student's present ability or achievement level in vocabulary, reading comprehension, quantitative reasoning, logic, and general information. General information is important when a teacher uses analogies and metaphors for learning purposes. Thorndike, et al.(1991) state that the difference between an aptitude and an achievement test is one "of degree and not one of kind." An aptitude test typically measures the more permanent effects of education and is used for predicting success in future learning situations. In contrast, an achievement test measures the more specific effects of instruction in the short term.

So at any point in time, a student is characterized by an aptitude vector(V_i) whose elements increase as a student progresses in education. The elements can be either skill-focused or factual-knowledge-focused. This vector is important for determining the optimal method of instruction for the ith student throughout time. The primary flaw of the orthodox economic theory of learning is that it is too static to accommodate the feedback loop for how present learning increases the elements in V_i and thus influences future learning.

In order to maximize the average learning rate for the class, the teacher must select a text and design a lesson/lecture that best "fits" or "matches" the students' aptitudes. In conventional classrooms, the teacher or school selects a single aptitude level to target. It might be the mean or median aptitude of the class or it may be selected on mere habit or convenience irrelevant of student characteristics. Whatever the selection process, the single aptitude vector selected is defined as the instructional target(3.2):

$$(3.2) \quad V^* = (S_1^*, S_2^*, S_3^*, \dots S_j^*)$$

$V^* =$ instructional target; embodied in the sophistication of the texts and lectures.

$S_j^* =$ assumed aptitude score on the jth aptitude test.

$$j = 1,2,3, \dots m$$

The m aptitudes are assumed relevant and equally important pre-requisites for the course of study. At a minimum, reading aptitude must be considered. Given this instructional target, which is implicit in the curriculum to be employed in the single classroom, some pupils will derive more benefit from the course than others, depending on their personal aptitude or current state of intellectual development.

More specifically, with student aptitude(3.1) and class instructional target(3.2) defined, *instructional error* for the ith student is vector 3.1 minus vector 3.2:

$$(3.3) \quad E_i = V_i - V^* = (S_{1i} - S_1^*, S_{2i} - S_2^*, S_{3i} - S_3^*, \dots S_{ji} - S_j^*)$$

where:

$E_i =$ instructional error vector for ith student
$V_i =$ ith pupil's aptitude vector(3.1)
$V^* =$ instructional target(3.2)

The instructional error vector(E_i)(3.3) is a one by j vector whose elements can be negative, positive, or zero. To the extent the element is positive, the course is too elementary and thus redundant for the ith student on that particular aptitude assumption. To the extent it is negative, the course is too difficult and thus overwhelming with respect to the jth aptitude. With respect to negative instructional error, Carroll(1963) explains that the more inferences a student is forced to make due to the fact that unfamiliar words and concepts go unexplained, the lower the rate of learning. In other words, the lectures/readings become unintelligible in proportion to the level of negative instructional error. Now if the element is zero, the instructor's assumed aptitude is equal to the ith student's aptitude and therefore approaches the optimality of a tutorial. No matter whether the element is positive or negative, it contributes to a lower rate of learning.[1]

Analyzing every element in every student's instructional error vector can be cumbersome. To simplify the analysis, a single, composite measure of instructional error for the ith student can be obtained by calculating the length or norm of the instructional error vector(3.4):

$$(3.4) \quad ||E_i|| = ||V_i - V^*|| = \sqrt{(E_i E_i')} = \sqrt{(V_i - V^*)(V_i - V^*)'} \geq 0$$

where:

$||E_i||$ = norm of instructional error vector for ith pupil

This scalar, non-negative, measure of instructional error is larger the more non-zero elements in the instructional error vector and the larger the absolute value of each element. If the aptitude vector is one-dimensional, measuring only reading aptitude for example, then the norm of the instructional error vector is simply the absolute value between the ith student's reading aptitude and the assumed reading-aptitude of the class. More generally, the norm of the instructional error vector measures the level of mis-match between the ith student's aptitude and the curriculum offered the student within the given classroom. To take an extreme example, if a course was taught in English to pupils who knew only the Spanish language, then the vocabulary and reading elements of the instructional error vector would make the composite measure of instructional error quite high. This would in turn cause the students' learning rates to approach zero. So finally, it is concluded that larger magnitudes of instructional error cause large decreases in learning rates just as small or subtle levels of instructional error cause relatively smaller decreases in learning rates.

To summarize, the tutorial expression for learning capital derived in the previous chapter(2.13) must yield to a more complicated classroom expression that accomodates instructional error and budget-sharing into the calculus. Again, the primary benefit of the classroom model of education is that teacher costs can be shared by the N pupil/families in the class. In other words, the classroom budget becomes equal to expenditures per-pupil(e) scaled up by the number of pupils in the class(N). The total classroom budget is observed in the numerator as eN within the classroom model(3.5) below:

(from 2.13) tutorial model: $$K_i = \frac{e}{c}$$

(3.5) classroom model: $$K_i = \frac{eN}{c + \beta||V_i - V^*||}$$

where:

K_i = average rate of learning for the ith pupil
e = average expenditures per-pupil/family
N = number of pupils in classroom
c = cost per-unit of learning capital for pupil(s) having zero instructional error
β = positive parameter to be statistically estimated that translates instructional error into dollars
V_i = ith pupil's aptitude vector
V^* = instructional target; embodied in the sophistication of course texts and lectures.

Notice how the classroom model(3.5) contrasts with the tutorial model(2.13) derived in the previous chapter. The total budget in the tutorial model was merely expenditures per-pupil(e) multiplied by one since there was only one pupil/family in the hypothetical, tutorial classroom(N = 1). It must be recognized that e does not necessarily remain constant in the transition from the tutorial to the classroom model of education. An increase in N is likely to be coupled with a decrease in e. Perhaps pupil/families desire expenditure relief or a reduction in e once a critical mass of funding is attained within a classroom whose budget is scaled up by N. Nonetheless, e is still expenditures per-pupil in both models. The financial burden of each pupil/family in attaining a sufficiently large classroom budget for the purpose of attracting a quality teacher can be reduced with classroom or group learning. So under conditions of zero instructional error for all N pupils within a classroom, a teacher's lecture can be interpreted as a non-rival, public good. The costs are shared and pupils' learning rates are high and equal since the curriculum is optimal for each and every pupil.

However, once again, the potential cost of classroom learning is that *instructional error* becomes a problem if pupils within a classroom have heterogeneous aptitudes. Notice that in the classroom model(3.5) for K_i, there now exists two components to the cost per-unit of learning capital appearing in the denominator for each individual pupil. c is the cost per-unit for the fortunate student(s) not experiencing any instructional error. Since the fortunate student's(s') aptitude vector is also the vector targeted for instruction, the instructional error expression vanishes and classroom instruction is similar to a tutorial in that the only costs are c dollars per-unit of learning capital. For the more unfortunate pupil(s) experiencing instructional error, additional costs are accumulated on top of c. These additional costs rise in proportion to the unique level of instructional error suffered by an individual pupil. This positive proportion is measured by β. Finally, with the presence of instructional error in the denominator of 3.5, the teacher's service as delivered through the verbal and written curriculum becomes a more rival good or a more private good. Each pupil/family's expenditure may be equal but each pupil's benefit or rate of learning differs due to differential levels of instructional error.

The important item to note concerning equation 3.5 is that a low and a high-aptitude pupil can potentially have the same learning rate if only the instructional target was set equal to their unique aptitude. This is a bold yet empirically supported idea that contradicts element one of the orthodox economic theory of learning.[2] In the orthodox model, instructional targets are either ignored or are assumed exogenous and fixed, perhaps in the name of maintaining "high academic standards." In many empirical studies, a positive association is found between pre-test scores(V_i) and learning rates(K_i) during the course. Typically, it is explained that higher-aptitude students, as measured by pre-test scores, have higher "intellectual capacity" or that their prior education has better prepared them to transform their study time into cognitive growth.

But the role of the instructional target being biased in favor of higher-achievers and thus *causing* a higher learning rate for higher-aptitude pupils is ignored. The student must adjust to the curriculum, not vice versa. Surely a teacher could make the learning rates relatively higher for pupils with lower pre-test scores by scaling the sophistication of the course downward. This would make the curriculum more optimal for lower-aptitude pupils but redundant for higher-aptitude pupils. Paradoxically, this would make learning rates *higher* for those pupils with the *lower* aptitudes or pre-test scores. Hence, it is necessary to sharply distinguish between learning rates and aptitudes as asserted in chapter one. A pupil's rate of learning is not and cannot be a proxy for some notion of natural or innate intellectual ability. The learning rate depends on the effectiveness of communication more than the pupil's physiological constitution.

The assumption of permanent, differential, and naturally-endowed learning rates within the orthodox economic theory of learning has perhaps been an expedient for mathematical and statistical modeling. For this position has not always been representative of the economics profession:

> Consider how nearly equal all men are in their bodily force, and even in their mental powers and faculties, ere[before] cultivated by education.
> - David Hume "Of the Original Contract," in *Essays, Moral and Political*, 1748, p. 291

> The difference of natural talents in different men is, in reality, much less than we are aware of... . The difference between the most dissimilar characters, between a philosopher and a common street porter, for example, seems to arise not so much from nature, as from habit, custom, and education. When they came into the world, and for the first six or eight years of their existence, they were, perhaps, very much alike, and neither their parents nor playfellows could perceive any remarkable difference.
> - Adam Smith *An Inquiry into the Nature and Causes of the Wealth of Nations*, 1776, p. 15

The important point is that a pupil's learning rate depends on how well the pupil's aptitude matches the sophistication of the curriculum. In other words, the rate of learning is socially determined. It does not depend on a pupil's aptitude viewed in isolation(V_i); but rather, the relative positioning or difference between the pupil's aptitude(V_i) and the instructional target($V*$).[3] And most interesting for educational policy, the sophistication or intensity of the curriculum is adjustable. It is a decision made by the educational suppliers - teachers and school administrators. To summarize, the theory of instructional error or more generally, learning capital, accounts for the quality of the pupil-teacher interaction which has been theoretically ignored in traditional specifications of the educational production function.

3.2   Pareto Optimal Instruction

Since the school controls the instructional target($V*$) with the selection of textbooks and the design of lectures, it determines the level and distribution of learning capital among the students who may all be paying the same tuition. Certainly, the instructional target should be made more sophisticated or more elementary if it increases the learning rate for all students. To appreciate this, assume that three groups of an equal number of students($N/3$) in the same classroom are each characterized by a unique, two-dimensional aptitude vector(a,b,c) as illustrated in figure 3.1.

Each group desires for the instructional target to be nearest their personal aptitude coordinates in figure 3.1 in order to have the lowest instructional error and thus highest learning rate. To review, the distance between the instructional target and a pupil's aptitude coordinates in figure 3.1 is the length or norm of the instructional error vector. If the course is designed for aptitudes $V*$, then the course is too elementary or redundant for all students.[4] If it is designed for $V***$, then it is too sophisticated or overwhelming for the entire class. The learning rate would increase for all three groups if the course content was made more($V*$) or less($V***$) rigorous. These adjustments would be illustrated by moving the instructional target toward the triangle(abc).

Perhaps the art of teaching is identifying and empathizing with the pupils' mode of thought or, in other words, discovering the students' aptitude space and responding appropriately. In short, there

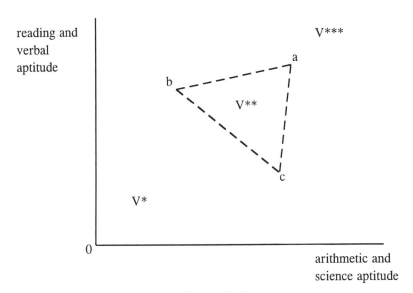

Figure 3.1
*Three, Two-Dimensional, Aptitude Vectors and a Graphical
Depiction of the Pareto-Optimal Instructional Space*

exist three elements necessary for quality instruction: 1) Teacher competence in subject matter, 2) Teacher knowledge of the aptitudes(V_i's) of all pupils to be taught, and 3) Teacher provision of appropriate vocabulary, metaphors, analogies, questions, and demonstrations that effectively delivers pupils from their familiar thoughts to new knowledge of subject matter(or minimize $\|V_i - V^*\|$).

Given all this, a theory of pareto optimal instruction is now offered. Any instructional target outside the triangle in figure 3.1 is pareto inferior. All students can be made better off by moving the instructional target toward the aptitude field illustrated by the triangle abc. The theory can be stated precisely using equation 3.5. In a single classroom characterized by a fixed budget(eN) and fixed value for c, a pareto change in the instructional target reduces the instructional error expression appearing in the denominator for all N students. As a result, the complete expression for the cost *per-unit* of learning capital appearing in the denominator decreases for all N students. This results in a higher learning rate(K_i) for each and every student in a common classroom. Given that the instructional target is and remains pareto optimal(V** in figure 3.1), any incremental change of the target is re-distributional. The optimal location of a pareto optimal instructional target within the triangle would depend on the relative weights assigned to students in a social welfare function.

An alternative way of viewing the instructional error problem is the following. With a pareto-optimal instructional target fixed(V** in figure 3.1), the larger the dispersion of aptitudes surrounding the instructional target in all directions, the larger the aggregate instructional error. This is an index for the level of redundancy and confusion within a single classroom. Notice that just because the instructional target is pareto optimal, it does not follow that instructional error is eliminated. Instructional error remains a problem. For the higher the aggregate instructional error in the classroom, the larger the average value for the instructional error expression in the denominator of equation 3.5. This translates into a lower rate of learning(K_i), on the average, for the class. So even with a pareto-optimal instructional target, the larger the dispersion of aptitudes within a single classroom, the less learning that occurs on the average.[5] In conclusion, the analysis thus far has focused on learning within a single classroom characterized by a single classroom budget and single instructional target.

3.3 Ability Tracking

A common strategy used to minimize aggregate instructional error and thus eliminate the low rates of learning is to divide the students into groups according to their present aptitudes.[6] Special programs such as remedial and accelerated tracking are instituted. Using the analysis accompanying figure 3.1, three separate programs of study might be created to satisfy the unique needs of the students(a,b,c). In other words, three separate tracks and corresponding curriculums are created for the group. Once divided, a unique, pareto optimal instructional target is employed for each of the three groups. In the example above, aggregate instructional error is eliminated with three tracks. However, under more realistic conditions, the aptitudes would not be distributed in a discreet fashion but continuously across the aptitude space. Hence, aggregate instructional error would be mitigated, not eliminated, unless a complete tutorial model was implemented.

The problem with this tracking policy is that it requires more resources due to the necessity of hiring more teachers. Or alternatively, the given budget of money(eN) used to purchase teacher-time must now be shared among the different tracks. The single teacher previously employed to instruct only the single, large group must now spread her attention across three separate curriculum/classrooms. Even if the same general subject matter is being taught to the same number of pupils, each unique aptitude-group requires a unique lesson plan or curriculum that is specifically designed to interface with the pupils' unique aptitudes. The planning, preparation, and presentation of these additional curricula is costly in terms of teacher attention. In other words, it is much less time consuming to teach three classes of the same subject matter while employing the same instructional target than it is to teach three classes of the same subject matter while employing three different instructional targets. This is why teachers are more concerned with the number of "preparations" assigned to them compared to the actual number of sections or classes.

The lesson to be drawn from this is that instructional targets(V^*'s) are scarce or expensive to supply. The efficiency windfall of sharing teacher costs within a relatively large, single aptitude-track with one instructional target, no matter the number of physical classrooms, begins to vanish as instruction is increasingly characterized by the more costly tutorial model that would be characterized by N curricula in the extreme. To formalize this, the expression for the amount of learning capital enjoyed by the ith student is once again altered in order to account for this tracking policy(3.6). The only difference between the original classroom equation(3.5) and equation 3.6 below is that the proportional variable, θ_i, is added.

$$(3.6) \quad K_i = \frac{eN\theta_i}{c + \beta\|V_i - V^*\|}$$

where:

θ_i = share of total school budget allocated to ith student's aptitude track. It is assumed that administrative expenditures are equally shared. Notice that pupils

enrolled in the same track enjoy the same and equal
share of the school's budget.

e = average educational expenditures per-pupil/family over
instructional time period

N = *total* school enrollment

c = cost per-unit of learning capital for pupil(s) with zero
instructional error in ith pupil's track

β = positive parameter to be statistically estimated that
translates instructional error into dollars

V_i = ith pupil's aptitude vector

V* = instructional target in ith pupil's track

So with tracking, funds are siphoned from the ith student's program
of study. Spending within the ith pupil's aptitude track decreased
from eN to $eN\theta_i$. Since funds are siphoned, teacher attention
necessarily decreases. This directly lowers the learning capital
available for the ith student due to a lower budget within the ith
student's track. The siphoned funds could have been used for
expenditure relief as well. Further notice that $eN(1 - \theta_i)$ is being
spent on all the remaining tracks within the larger school. The more
tracks in the school the lower the share of the school budget within
each track. Hence, each aptitude-track within a large school can be
interpreted as a "school-within-a-school" with its own budget($eN\theta_i$)
and unique instructional target(V*). Most important, adding the
proportional variable(θ_i) in equation 3.6 makes the learning-capital
expression(K_i) relevant for school-level efficiency analysis if N is
now interpreted as total school enrollment rather than classroom
enrollment.

Given that V* remained constant in the ith pupil's track, the initial
K_i that existed prior to tracking can be retrieved only by raising the
overall school budget sufficiently in order to compensate for the
siphoning of $eN(1 - \theta_i)$ funds from the ith pupil's track. This leads to
the economic dilemma encountered with instructional error. Each
family is not only concerned with their child's absolute rate of learning
but also the expenditures necessary to obtain it. The cost per-unit of
learning capital for a particular school increases with heterogeneous
aptitudes. Either instructional error and the denominator remains
high in a single track or θ_i becomes less than one in the numerator
due to the necessity of sharing the given school budget. In other

words, a fixed school budget simply will not go as far in producing a high average K_i in a school the more heterogeneous the aptitudes.

Again, it is important to acknowledge that the average value for θ_i decreases with the number of aptitude tracks. On the other hand, the share of the school's budget being awarded to the ith pupil's track depends on the school's budgetary politics. Thus, the N pupils characterized by heterogeneous aptitudes have conflicts of interest. They compete for the single instructional target(V^*) *within* a track and/or for a larger share(θ_i) of the school budget *between* tracks. The larger a track's budget, the more talented teachers and more aptitude-specific courses enjoyed by the pupils within the track. One student's gain can become another student's loss with respect to the allocation of V^* and θ_i.[7]

To summarize as well as include the opportunity costs of learning capital in the model, let τ_i be the fraction of the school's budget paid by the ith family. The ith family's educational expenditures per-instructional period is then equal to $eN\tau_i$. In a public school, τ_i would depend on the family's relative tax burden. In a private school, it would depend on tuition and financial aid policy.[8] It is uncertain whether a school's budgetary process would or even should insure that the amount allocated to a pupil within a school is proportional to the amount the pupil/family contributed to the school. Given all this, if K_i(3.6) is divided by family educational expenditures($eN\tau_i$), then output per-dollar spent for the ith pupil/family is the new and more revealing expression(3.7):

$$(3.7) \quad \frac{K_i}{eN\tau_i} = \left\{\frac{1}{eN\tau_i}\right\} \frac{eN\theta_i}{c + \beta\|V_i - V^*\|} = \frac{\theta_i}{\tau_i\{c + \beta\|V_i - V^*\|\}}$$

where:

$K_i = q_i/T_i$ = average rate of learning for ith pupil

e = average educational expenditures per-pupil/family over instructional time period

N = total school enrollment

τ_i = share of total school expenditures borne by ith pupil/family

θ_i = share of total school budget allocated to ith pupil's track

c = cost per-unit of learning capital for pupil(s) with zero instructional error in ith pupil's track

β = positive parameter to be statistically estimated that translates instructional error into dollars

V_i = ith pupil's aptitude vector

V^* = instructional target in ith pupil's track

Equation 3.7 describes the average performance of a school in transforming family expenditures($eN\tau_i$) into learning capital(K_i) for the ith pupil. The larger the value for $K_i/eN\tau_i$, the more efficient is the school from an individual family's perspective. The inverse of 3.7 is the price per-unit of learning capital for the ith pupil/family. With a given expenditure level for the ith pupil/family, the higher the price the lower the rate of learning. In other words, the inverse of 3.7 is the financial opportunity cost for a unit of intellectual growth given that T_i is fixed.

In the next chapter, equation 3.7 is analyzed in more detail. The important question to be addressed is: Who is responsible for each of the variables appearing in equation 3.7 and how might the variables be manipulated in order to promote higher mean cognitive growth and equality within the typical school with a given budget? As will be seen, the expression contains rich policy implications for the effective management of a nation's common schools.

Notes

1   An example of how a student might simultaneously suffer from both positive and negative instructional error is offered. Suppose a student has a sophisticated vocabulary but is unfamiliar with calculus. An economics course using calculus concepts combined with an elementary vocabulary and reading level would impose positive instructional error in math aptitude and negative instructional error in vocabulary and reading aptitude.

2   For a more detailed empirical and theoretical defense of this statement see Bloom(1976), Block(1974), and their colleagues'(Arlin, 1973; Anderson, 1976; T. Levin, 1975; Azcelik, 1974; Cronbach and Snow, 1977) work under the general theme of Mastery Learning. The general conclusion of this work is that when lower aptitude students are provided remedial help in order to master pre-requisites for a course, their rates of learning become equalized with initially higher aptitude peers on future learning tasks. This leads to the conclusion that the rate of learning is dependent more on the interaction of present instructional targets and historical learning rather than on genetics and physiology. This also explains why psychologists are hard-pressed to distinguish between aptitude and achievement tests(Thorndike, et. al.; 1991).

    See Vernon(1987) for a more recent survey on the heredity-environmental debate for the determinants of intelligence. In Vernon's survey, notice that there is no discussion on how historical learning and present instructional targets influence the learning rate and therefore overall cognitive achievement growth and acquired abilities.

3   A short digression is necessary concerning this conclusion. The legitimate physiological concept of "learning handicap" has perhaps been broadly defined to also include pupils with an aptitude vector(V_i) lower than the peers in their grade cohort as well as lower than the instructional target offered the cohort. Due to the pupils' relatively lower learning rates due to this negative instructional error, they are frequently labeled as "slow-learners" as if it were due to some physical deficiency. But this is false. It is due to a sub-optimal instructional target on the supply-side of education.

    Alternatively, these pupils are often labeled as having a "deficit attention span" as if it were due to a culturally-determined restlessness or unruliness. But would not any normal pupil become restless if the curriculum offered is consistently and persistently unintelligible due to high instructional error? To conclude, the notion of a "learning handicap" is a relative concept and becomes less meaningful the larger the proportion of pupils that are alleged to have one. As soon as the majority of pupils are concluded to have a similar learning handicap, they are no longer handicapped since they are now the norm. See Rosenbaum(1976) for a theme similar to this footnote. He finds the psychologist's notion of IQ to be highly problematic as a measure to assess natural intellectual endowment or ability to benefit from formal instruction. He also provides quotes from psychologists who admit serious problems with the IQ concept.

4   This problem is discussed in two reports by the U.S. Department of Education: 1) "A recent study by Education Products Information Exchange revealed that a majority of students were able to master 80% of the material in some of their subject matter texts before they had even opened the books. Many books do not challenge the students to whom they are assigned." *A Nation At Risk: The Imperative for Educational Reform*(National Commission on Excellence in Education, 1983). 2) "Gifted and talented elementary school students have mastered from 35 to 50 percent of the curriculum to be offered in five basic subjects before they begin the school year." *National Excellence: A Case for Developing America's Talent*(U.S. Dept. of Education; October, 1993).

5   Note that a student may be experiencing a very low rate of learning due to high instructional error and still not fail a course nor even receive a low grade. The student is merely being evaluated on their previous stock of knowledge(A_i) and not on their achievement growth(q_i). They may also be going through the motions of homework or putting in large amounts of time-on-task(T_i) in order to satisfy course requirements while enjoying minimal cognitive growth.

It is also important to emphasize that the reviewing of cognitive material is important. But a distinction between review and redundancy must be recognized. Similarly, challenging students with an always elusive instructional target may be important. But a distinction between challenging and overwhelming students must be recognized. The extreme statements are made in order to simplify and thus analyze the fundamental forces causing efficiency.

6   The effect of tracking on a student's achievement has received a large amount of attention from educational researchers. The conclusion seems to be that being placed in a lower aptitude track is a self-fulfilling prophecy due to lower standards of achievement in lower aptitude tracks. See Hallinan(1994) for a brief essay on this subject.

7   There seems to be a potential for zero-sum rent-seeking behavior using the "voice" mechanism in petitioning a school for changing the budget allocation *between* tracks and the instructional targets *within* tracks(Hirschman,1970). This voice-mechanism becomes quite literal

when a pupil alters the agenda within a classroom by asking questions that has the effect of re-focusing the oral curriculum or instructional target(V^*) toward the pupil's personal aptitude(V_i).

8   If τ_i was summed up across all N family's in a particular school, it may not equal one. This may be due to expenditures coming from sources other than direct family educational expenditures such as intergovernmental grants, endowment income, or gifts.

Chapter IV

Implications of the Theory
of Learning Capital

The goal in theorizing about educational production is to isolate the relative contributions of the school and the student in producing cognitive achievement growth in a formal school setting. This is necessary in order to diagnose the possible source of stagnating test scores within primary and secondary education so that a possible cure might become evident. The contributions of the school and student were theoretically isolated in the tutorial model. However, the unique influences of the school and student have not been isolated within the classroom model.

In order to isolate the relative contributions within the classroom model, the output per-dollar ratio(3.7) derived in the previous chapter is altered in two ways. First, assume the expenditure burden is equally shared by all families within the hypothetical school which makes τ_i equal to 1/N. Second, by multiplying both sides of equation 3.7 by T_i we arrive at a more intuitive mathematical model of learning(4.1):

$$(4.1) \quad \frac{q_i}{e_i} = \left\{ \frac{\theta i N}{c + \beta || V_i - V^* ||} \right\} T_i$$

where:

q_i = cognitive achievement growth per-instructional period
e_i = educational expenditures per-pupil/family over instructional time period
θ_i = share of total school budget allocated to ith pupil's track
N = total school enrollment
c = cost per-unit of learning capital for pupil(s) with zero instructional error in ith pupil's track
β = positive parameter to be statistically estimated that translates instructional error into dollars
V_i = ith pupil's aptitude vector
V^* = instructional target in ith pupil's track
T_i = total time-on-task for ith pupil over instructional period

Suppose expenditures per-pupil(e_i) is given for a particular school. With e_i fixed and normalized, equation 4.1 is interpreted as a quasi-production function for the ith pupil's cognitive achievement growth(q_i) in a formal school setting. The expression in brackets is the school's contribution to the ith student's cognitive growth. It is the amount of learning capital per-pupil expenditures(K_i/e_i) supplied to the ith pupil. The larger the bracketed expression the higher the pupil's learning rate and thus the better quality is the school for the ith pupil. Hence, the bracketed expression is interpreted as the supply-side of education. The demand-side of education remains intact in equation 4.1 since T_i is the student's contribution to his or her own cognitive growth. The higher a pupil's perseverance in time-on-task(T_i), the more dedicated is the pupil to intellectual growth.

So equation 4.1 serves three important functions. First, it normalizes and thus abstracts from the effect the absolute level of funding(e_i) has on cognitive growth(q_i). In other words, a quality school depends on deriving the highest learning rate from a given level of spending(K_i/e_i); not which school can spend the most. Second, it eliminates the theoretical ambiguity as to whether the pupil/family or the school is responsible for success or failure in cognitive growth. And finally, equation 4.1 is an average approximation for the marginal impact of funding($\partial q_i/\partial e_i$) within a school. To see this, multiply both sides of 4.1 by e_i and then take the derivative of q_i with respect to e_i. Recall that the marginal impact of funding has been found to be statistically no different from zero in most empirical studies(Hanushek, 1986, 1989).

Despite the fact that the relative contributions of the school and pupil/family have been theoretically isolated and can perhaps be empirically measured, producing large cognitive growth(q_i) still remains a cooperative effort. For if T_i approaches zero even the best school, as measured by a large bracketed expression in 4.1, has little impact on a pupil's cognitive growth. On the other hand, significant pupil effort, as measured by a high T_i, has little return in growth unless a school offers a high learning rate as measured by the bracketed expression: $(\theta_i N)/(c + \beta||V_i - V^*||)$. Hence, pupil effort and school quality are both necessary but neither are sufficient in producing high intellectual growth.

Given equation 4.1, it is unlikely that a pupil would persevere in high levels of T_i if the pupil senses that the bracketed expression or the rate of learning is almost nil. Metaphorically, a pupil will not jump onto the educational wagon if it is not going to move. Hence, there is likely to be a positive, causal relation extending from the bracketed expression to T_i even though this will not be formally recognized in the mathematics. As an empirical observation, this might be seen by a pupil not enrolling in a course that is either too elementary and thus redundant or too difficult and thus overwhelming.

If a family could choose a school, the pupil/family is expected to choose that school with the largest value for $(\theta_i N)/(c + \beta||V_i - V^*||)$. For example, under a voucher scheme, e_i appearing in equation 4.1 would be the redemption value for the ith pupil/family's voucher. They would choose the school providing the most learning from their given time and money. In other words, the pupil/family would engage in a neighborhood or perhaps a more global search for a school offering the maximum level for $(\theta_i N)/(c + \beta||V_i - V^*||)$ as seen in equation 4.1.

On a more concrete level, what school characteristics might attract a pupil/family? Previously, it has been recommended that a pupil/family should choose a school having a student body of relatively high mean aptitude(Henderson, Mieszkowski, and Sauvageau, 1978; Murnane, 1984; Arnott and Rowse, 1987) or high mean socio-economic status(Chubb and Moe, 1990; Gyimah-Brempong and Gyapong, 1991). This is because individual student achievement growth has been found to be positively associated with these mean characteristics of a student's peers. The rationale is that the individual pupil has better quality pupils to interact with and perhaps teacher morale is higher within these schools.

But upon examining the bracketed expression in equation 4.1, this action might hurt a pupil. For example, enrolling in a school with peers of relatively higher initial achievement would likely result in an overwhelming curriculum being imposed upon the pupil ($\|V_i < V^*\|$). This causes a low learning rate in the initial phases of instruction due to having overwhelming and thus unintelligible lectures and texts. Also, the learning rate will approach zero over time due to the pupil's peers progressing much faster equipped with their relatively higher learning rates due to their lower instructional error.

Given the theory of learning capital(4.1), it may be more important to find a student body with similar and homogeneous aptitudes rather than relatively higher mean aptitudes. This behavior improves the chance of a pupil enjoying minimal instructional error while also not having the school budget dispersed over many competing aptitude tracks. To support this assertion, in chapter six it is demonstrated that the alleged peer effect, as traditionally measured by average student-body characteristics, is merely spuriously correlated with more fundamental and previously omitted empirical variables measuring the instructional error phenomenon. In other words, high achievement growth is not caused by the high mean aptitude or high mean socio-economic status of a school. Rather, high achievement growth is caused by a low dispersion of aptitudes in a school. Coincidentally, the schools having a low dispersion of aptitudes also have a high mean aptitude and high mean socio-economic status.

A final comment is necessary concerning the relative contributions of the school and pupil isolated in equation 4.1. The teacher/school exercises some influence on a pupil's T_i by controlling the pace at which V^* increases throughout the instructional period. Instructional-error costs are imposed on pupils not keeping their V_i equal to V^* by adjusting T_i appropriately. K_i decreases for pupils falling behind or ambitious students proceeding ahead of V^*. For example, if a lecture proceeds on the assumption that pupils read the assigned readings, then the learning rate is high for those pupils who really did the readings assigned prior to the lecture. On the other hand, the rate of learning is quite low for those students neglecting to prepare since many concepts and allusions are unfamiliar. Hence, consistent studying may be just as important if not more important as long periods of studying. Nevertheless, a quality school depends on how flexible the school is in responding to a pupil's level of preparation or current aptitude as measured by V_i no matter whether the instructional period is measured in hours, days, or years.[1]

4.1 The Elusive Goal of Equality of Opportunity

At this point a digression is necessary to discuss the concept of "equality of opportunity" in the context of the theory of learning capital. Recall that this is the second common school goal. It is satisfied when the school's contribution to achievement growth, as expressed by $(\theta_i N)/(c + \beta||V_i - V^*||)$ within equation 4.1, is equal for all N students within a school. If perfect equality of opportunity is achieved, then differential cognitive growth levels among students can be attributed entirely to differential levels of student effort or time-on-task(T_i). In this ideal world the pupil/family is more responsible for its level of cognitive achievement on graduation day. This would, in turn, make income inequality based on inequality in accumulated human capital(A_i) more acceptable.

However, heterogeneous aptitudes, differential T_i's, and a small and fixed budget(e_i) make it improbable for a school to provide *both* a reasonably high learning rate for every pupil along with equality of opportunity. In a school with large classrooms coupled with diverse aptitudes within the classrooms, the phrase "equality of opportunity" denies the fact of scarce resources or similarly, limited instructional targets. Given a single instructional target in a classroom filled with pupils of heterogeneous aptitude, equality of learning rates is impossible.

Equality of learning rates could very well be achieved by providing a unique written/oral curriculum for each and every pupil of unique aptitude. But providing this equality on a consistent and daily basis requires slicing the teaching staff's total time into trivially small subsets for each pupil. The teachers' time is spent both preparing the numerous curriculums as well as communicating it to each pupil. Under these conditions, the typical pupil might have quality teacher-pupil interaction for only a small fraction of a school day. In mathematical terms, θ_i becomes quite small.

So from a static perspective, heterogeneous aptitudes in a school impairs a school's ability to offer a high learning rate for every pupil when constrained by a fixed and small budget of money and thus teacher time. This depressed average learning rate will persist no matter whether a few fortunate pupils enjoy high learning rates at the expense of their peers or whether all pupils enjoy a small yet equal learning rate. This depressed average school learning rate does not follow from scarcity of "intellectual capacity" at the lower achievement levels. It follows from scarcity of instructional targets and variety in current achievement levels.

From this, one becomes more sensitive to the public school administrators' insatiable appetite for funding given that they are charged to provide high and equal learning rates for their pupils. In order to provide reasonably high and equal learning rates under conditions of extreme aptitude diversity, the administrator may have to assign a single public-school teacher to each individual pupil for the duration of each school day. However, each public school teacher presently costs \$36,933 per year.[2] Most pupil/families are neither able nor willing to pay \$36,933 in annual tuition-tax to permit this. Obviously, there are economies of group learning due to the ability to share teacher costs in a common classroom and thus keep tuition/ tax or e_i reasonably low.

Given all this, the dual goals of high and equal learning rates may not be as bleak as this static model suggests. This issue is re-visited after discussing how a school administrator might maximize the mean value for $(\theta_i N)/(c + \beta||V_i - V^*||)$ within a single school and thus do the best they can with given resources. By maximizing $(\theta_i N)/(c + \beta||V_i - V^*||)$ for the representative pupil, the school indirectly maximizes the mean q_i/e_i for a school(4.1) which is the first common school goal.

4.2 The Elements of School Efficiency

So what are the determinants of average school efficiency and therefore school excellence? Or how are pupil/families to be guaranteed a high mean or expected learning rate per-pupil expenditures within a school? To answer this, the individual elements contained within the bracketed expression of equation 4.1 are analyzed in detail. In order to maximize $(\theta_i N)/(c + \beta \| V_i - V^* \|)$, the cost per-unit of learning capital appearing in the denominator must be minimized while the numerator must be maximized.

To begin, c is a cost-effective ratio that accounts for all non-instructional-error efficiencies. In other words, it measures the performance of a school in transforming funding into learning capital within the ith student's track for the targeted student(s) having zero instructional error. The most straightforward technique for minimizing c is to employ educational inputs having the highest marginal product per-dollar as a track's budget is expanded. For example, a teacher development workshop might have a higher marginal product per-dollar compared to the purchasing of supplemental textbooks. Again, as argued in the tutorial chapter, the lower c the better quality is the school:

$$(4.2) \quad c = \frac{eN\theta_i}{K^*}$$

c measures how well the school solves the constrained maximization of K* within the ith pupil's track:

$$(4.3) \quad L = K^*(x_1, x_2, x_3, \ldots x_m) - \lambda(eN\theta_i - p_1 x_1 - p_2 x_2 - \ldots p_m x_m)$$

where:

K^* = average learning rate for targeted pupil(s) in ith pupil's track. The asterisk denotes the rate of learning under conditions of zero instructional error.

c = cost per-unit of learning capital for pupil(s) with zero instructional error in ith pupil's track

x_j = educational input; $j = 1, 2, \ldots m$

p_j = price of jth educational input; $j = 1, 2, \ldots m$

e = average pupil/family expenditures

λ = Lagrangian multiplier

θ_i = share of total school budget allocated to ith pupil's track

N = total school enrollment

Both input prices and technology are embedded in c. It is determined primarily by the academic competence, management skill, and salaries of school personnel since education is a labor-intensive industry. Why is academic competence important for minimizing c? Suppose a teacher or textbook author is ignorant of the theoretical principles to be taught in a course. The intellectual growth, even for the targeted pupil(s), becomes negligible in proportion to the level of ignorance of the teacher or author. It is assumed, by the way, that the standardized test used to measure progress is in fact measuring the extent to which the correct theory is being learned. A teacher or author who does not know the correct theory is unable to communicate it to the pupil. Large amounts of time-on-task(T_i) cannot overcome this problem. The learning rate(K^*) approaches zero which causes c to approach infinity which causes q_i to approach zero.

There are several additional factors influencing c. c is expected to be smaller for Catholic schools who benefit from priests, nuns, and brothers contributing some of their teaching services for free. These contributed services increase K^* but not $eN\theta_i$. Third, c is expected to increase with the size of a school's bureaucracy. A definition for bureaucracy would be a staff position that dramatically increases $eN\theta_i$ while having little impact in raising K^*. Fourth, a school nutrition program may even be optimal for minimizing c, especially if the targeted student does not eat breakfast at home. It would also be kept high with the optimal scheduling of study breaks. Sixth, c is expected to increase with the level of funding within a track due to diminishing returns to expenditures. Even the targeted pupil is unable to master organic chemistry in one hour if only a sufficient amount of expenditures were made. Finally and to a far lesser extent, c depends on the number and prices of textbooks, desks, physical plant, maintenance, etc. As a result of these final two items, c is likely to rise in proportion to school enrollment(N). c is now referred to as *c-efficiency*.

In addition to c, notice that N appears in the numerator of $(\theta_i N)/(c + \beta || V_i - V^* ||)$. The implication is that, ceteris paribus, there are economies of scale with respect to school enrollment due to the school's per-pupil budget(e_i) being scaled up by N. However, as discussed, it is likely that c, within the denominator, is positively related to N. So enrollment(N) is expected to increase both the numerator and the denominator and therefore the effect of school size is theoretically indeterminate. Hence, the net effect of N on efficiency(q_i/e_i) must await empirical testing.

Next, and most important, a more detailed analysis of the instructional error expression appearing in the denominator of $(\theta_i N)/$ $(c + \beta||V_i - V*||)$ eventually leads to the conclusion that school efficiency depends on producing equality. The expected level of instructional error suffered by a pupil within a school can be calculated by taking the arithmetic mean of instructional error for all N students within the school:

(4.4)

$$\mu = \frac{\beta||V_1 - V*|| + \beta||V_2 - V*|| + \beta||V_3 - V*|| + ...\beta||V_N - V*||}{N}$$

or

$$\mu = \frac{\beta}{N} \sum_{i=1}^{N} ||V_i - V*||$$

where:

μ = expected instructional error for the ith pupil within a single school having N pupils

N = total school enrollment

β = positive parameter to be statistically estimated that translates instructional error into dollars

V_i = ith pupil's aptitude vector

$V*$ = instructional target in ith pupil's track

The cost of expected instructional error$(\mu)(4.4)$ is accumulated on top of normal education costs(c) and is measured in dollars. As an empirical approximation, the aptitude vector(V_i) is interpreted as a single composite score on a battery of tests measuring the current stock of reasoning skills and factual-knowledge the ith student has for all school subjects.[3] This simplification makes the individual instructional error expression merely the absolute value between the ith pupil's pre-test score($V_i = a_i$) and the instructional target($V* = a*$). Thus, the level and distribution of past school outputs determine present school learning rates via expected instructional error. Unlike *c-efficiency*, which is always positive, any positive value for $\mu(4.4)$ is considered waste. Policy should be directed toward driving μ to zero. In other words, the difference between each and every pupil's aptitude vector(V_i) and their corresponding instructional target(V^*) should be eliminated. This is not a new idea:

> In regard to the ordinary management or administration of a school, how much judgment is demanded in the organization of classes, so that no scholar shall either be clogged and retarded, or hurried with an unequal yoke-fellow. Great discretion is necessary in the assignment of lessons, in order to avoid, on the one hand, such shortness in the tasks, as allows time to be idle; and, on the other, such over-assignment, as render thoroughness and accuracy impracticable, and thereby so habituate the pupil to mistakes and imperfections, that he cares little or nothing about committing them. Lessons, as far as it is possible, should be adjusted to the capacity of the scholar... The sense of shame, or of regret for ignorance, can never be made exquisitely keen, if the lessons given are so long, or so difficult, as to make failures frequent.
> - Horace Mann(1840), report to the Massachusetts Board of Education(as reported in Cremin,1957).

Parents think that on the whole they can do better in a more homogeneous class, where bright children are not there to take up the time of the teacher. Perhaps a slow child is not considered as threatening to the educational achievement of one's own child as a disruptive one who prevents the class from working. But we all know that parents often complain that the work is too easy or that it is oriented to the slower children or those who do not want to work too hard, and that many parents seek for a class or school in which their children will be challenged. As many parents seek for a school or class that is not too challenging and does not overwhelm their children. This is common parental behavior.
- Nathan Glazer(1983), professor of education and sociology.

Comparisons of language use in middle-income and lower-income families suggest that there may be a discontinuity between language of the home and the language of the school - especially for students from certain low-income and linguistic minority backgrounds... . Heath[1982] identified a mismatch between the language used in the home and the language demanded in the classroom. When the structure of discourse in the classroom corresponded to the pattern of discourse in the low-income home, students' academic performance improved.
- Hugh Mehan(1992), specialist in the sociology of language.

A major organizational problem in developing secondary school curriculum is how to accomodate the diversity in student's skills as they enter high school(p. 105)... Small schools with limited fiscal resources and where the majority of students typically entered poorly prepared had a particularly difficult time responding to the needs of the relatively few students capable of pursuing advanced work(p. 106-107).

> - Anthony S. Bryk, Valerie E. Lee, and Peter B. Holland
> *Catholic Schools and the Common Good*

Classroom teachers do little to accomodate the different learning needs of gifted children. In a large national survey, most teachers said they give the same assignments to both gifted and average students almost all the time, and few said they use many "higher level" teaching strategies in their classrooms.

> - U.S. Department of Education *National Excellence: A Case for Developing America's Talent*(October, 1993) p. 20

There are several techniques available to minimize $\mu(4.4)$ or average instructional error within a school and thus cure the problem articulated by the aforementioned authors. First, school personnel should insure V* is at least pareto optimal as discussed in the preceding chapter. Second, a school could offer many pareto-optimal instructional targets(V*'s) distributed throughout the aptitude space defined by the aptitude space of the student body. Students, with the help of counselors, would sort themselves around the instructional target most appropriate for their present aptitudes and thus minimize their instructional error and maximize their individual learning rates.

However, as acknowledged previously, the more instructional targets offered the lower the share(θ_i) of the total budget enjoyed by each pupil/family for the purpose of maximizing their respective K* within each track(4.3). For example, when twenty students are divided into two tracks, the teacher's time is also divided in half. Each curriculum becomes more intelligible for each group, but the time spent by the teacher in preparing and communicating a given curriculum is less. So an aggressive tracking policy does in fact lower the expected value for the instructional error expression(μ) in the denominator of $(\theta_i N)/(c + \beta \| V_i - V^* \|)$. However, this more aggressive tracking policy also lowers the average or expected value for θ_i in the numerator. Therefore, there may be little or zero net efficiency-gain from a policy of aptitude tracking.

4.3 *Selection Efficiency*

There is a superior or cheaper technique for minimizing μ(4.4) within a school. This technique avoids spreading the fixed budget too thinly across many tracks or expanding the overall budget. A school simply enrolls a student body with homogeneous aptitudes(V_i's) through the use of entrance examinations. This policy does not necessarily imply that the school will select the highest-aptitude students. A small dispersion of aptitudes can be selected from anywhere in the distribution. The school merely defines an aptitude niche for itself within a geographic-community's student population.

This minimum dispersion of V_i's permits a minimum level for μ *and* a maximum level for mean θ_i. This translates into a higher average rate of learning per-dollar(K_i/e_i) for the school. So with the selection of homogeneous aptitudes, the mean value for θ_i in the numerator of $(\theta_i N)/(c + \beta||V_i - V^*||)$ remains high while the expected instructional error(μ) in the denominator remains low. On a more general level, if average time-on-task(T_i) is constant, this efficient selection policy translates into a higher expected value for cognitive achievement growth per-dollar spent(q_i/e_i) as seen in equation 4.1.

It is believed that private schools do behave in this manner in order to compete efficiently. On the other hand, public schools must accept all students residing in their geographically-defined school district and therefore are legally constrained from pursuing this efficiency. This is believed to be one cause for the private school advantage in efficiency. Hence, the advantage is due to bad law, not the stereotyped lazy and overpaid government employee. In fact, the present policy makes the public teachers' jobs relatively more difficult since they have to spread their attention among more diverse aptitudes. Achieving more efficiency by enrolling students with homogeneous aptitudes is now called *selection efficiency*. So the first hypothesis to be tested in the empirical chapter is:

Hypothesis One: The expected value for q_i/e_i, which is a flow measure over an instructional time period, is negatively related to σ, the standard deviation of aptitudes for the ith student's school peers at the beginning of an instructional period, ceteris paribus.

4.4 Dynamic Efficiency

The general proposition that a lower dispersion of student aptitudes leads to greater efficiency finally leads to the most interesting conclusion of this work. Once a student body is enrolled in a given school, the more a school reduces the dispersion of student aptitudes in the present, the more efficient the school becomes in the future. This is true within each aptitude-track and is also true for the entire school. This conclusion should also be true no matter whether the instructional period is measured in hours, days, months, or years. So how can a school reduce aptitude dispersion in the present? It is absurd to think schools would attempt to strip high-aptitude students of some of their knowledge using surgical lobotomies for collapsing the upper-tail of the aptitude distribution.

The only method to minimize dispersion in the present and thus increase efficiency in the future is to concentrate a disproportionate amount of resources on lower-aptitude students. Again, the resources are:

1) θ_i: the time of teachers most skillful at maximizing K* and encouraging high T_i's.
2) V*: within each track or course, the instructional target should be biased toward the lowest V_i's.

For example, in the early stages of instruction, the school offers general math and basic English rather than calculus and advanced English when constrained by a fixed budget.

From this policy, the learning rate becomes greater for low-aptitude pupils compared to high-aptitude pupils. Now, to the extent that lower-aptitude students' time-on-task is equal or greater than higher-aptitude students' time-on-task, the dispersion of aptitudes or stock of achievement decreases and efficiency increases over time. In other words, successful remediation of lower-aptitude students eventually results in a higher expected q_i/e_i for all students within a school. This can be seen by collapsing the pareto instructional triangle(figure 3.1) by placing the instructional target(V*) in the southwest portion.

It may be the case that a school cannot decrease the dispersion over time due to the lower-aptitude students' lower perseverance level in time-on-task(T_i). However, the incentive remains to at least minimize the growth of dispersion or inequality. If producing equality causes more efficiency, then allowing more inequality exacerbates inefficiency. Therefore, the inference that more equality of achievement outcomes causes higher efficiency over time is a logically-supported, theoretical conclusion.

Increasing efficiency by producing equality of achievement outcomes could be accomplished through either political decree in a public school or simply through the use of market incentives to be efficient in a private school. The question of whether the state or market is more effective at providing equality *and thus* efficiency must await empirical analysis. The increase in efficiency that comes from the production of equality over time in order to minimize μ and maximize mean θ_i and thus maximize the expected learning per-dollar(q_i/e_i)(4.1) for a school is now called *dynamic efficiency*. So the second hypothesis to be tested in the empirical chapter is:

Hypothesis Two: The expected value for q_i/e_i, which is a flow measure over an instructional time period, is negatively related to $\Delta\sigma$, the change in the standard deviation of the aptitudes of the ith student's school peers during the same instructional time period, ceteris paribus.

To summarize, the three categories of *c-efficiency, selection efficiency,* and *dynamic efficiency* account for all possible efficiencies within a school over an instructional time period since the first is everything the latter two are not. As discussed, the latter two efficiency categories are ultimately linked to the underlying problem of instructional error. To the extent a school minimizes σ and $\Delta\sigma$, the school can increase the average level of cognitive growth(q_i) while maintaining a fixed level of expenditures per-pupil(e_i) and time-on-task per-pupil(T_i). Finally, recall that the efficient production of cognitive growth is not the only criterion for evaluating a school. The three common school goals are re-visited at this juncture:

1) Maximum average cognitive achievement growth per-dollar spent per-pupil. Or identically, maximum expected value for q_i/e_i within the school.

2) Equality of educational opportunity, or more strongly, a minimum $\Delta\sigma$ within the school.
3) Integration of students from different ethnic, racial, socio-economic, and handicap backgrounds.

Theoretically it has been argued that goal one is achieved to the extent that goal two is achieved due to the concept of *dynamic efficiency*. Hence, no conflict exists between efficiency and equality within a school. A school is excellent or efficient not *in spite* of being equal but rather, *because* of being equal. Thus, element two of the orthodox economic theory of learning has been theoretically contradicted. As a result, a profit-seeking school trying to attract or retain enrollment and thus revenue by offering a high expected rate of learning must produce equality or at least minimize the growth of inequality over time. Peculiar as it may seem, market forces may perhaps be well-suited for the production of high and equal cognitive achievement growth within a school when viewed from a dynamic or evolutionary perspective.

4.5 Tension Within the Common School Philosophy

The third common school goal of integration has been ignored up to this point. Encouraging children to love, respect, and understand others different from themselves is a noble and necessary social goal. The physical integration of pupils from diverse ethnic, racial, and socio-economic backgrounds is a necessary condition for furthering this goal.

However, unlike goals one and two, a tradeoff is likely to exist between common school goals one and three. Why is this so? It is a safe empirical generalization to conclude, for whatever reason; that Blacks, Hispanics, and students from low-income families score disproportionately lower than white, higher-income students on cognitive achievement tests at any point in time for a given cohort. So the more a school reflects the general population with respect to representation of the following categories: Blacks, Hispanics, socio-economic status, and learning handicaps; the larger the values for σ and $\Delta\sigma$ in the school. This is because racial, ethnic, handicap, and socio-economic diversity causes aptitude diversity due to differential historical learning and differential present rates for T_i. So, insofar as hypothesis one and two are true, then the following hypothesis logically follows and will be tested:

Hypothesis Three: The more a school is characterized by racial, ethnic, socio-economic, and handicap diversity; the lower the expected value for q_i/e_i within the school due to higher values for σ and $\Delta\sigma$, ceteris paribus.

Several comments are necessary concerning this third hypothesis. It may be the case that the cost in foregone mean q_i/e_i within a school may be worth the benefit of integrating the disadvantaged with advantaged students. Unless, of course, the foregone achievement growth is disproportionately borne by the disadvantaged because they are unable to get optimal instructional targets once integrated with higher-aptitude students. With a fixed budget or fixed number of instructional targets, somebody must inevitably suffer a lower K_i and thus q_i when σ and $\Delta\sigma$ increase. It may be wishful thinking that the costs would be borne equally among all pupils. Thus, integrating pupils may result in a more insidious form of discrimination and inequality *if* instructional targets are maintained for higher-aptitude pupils.

Placing a low-aptitude, minority pupil in a class beside a white, higher-aptitude pupil does not result in intellectual osmosis or the higher-aptitude pupil somehow raising the lower-aptitude pupil's growth rate in mathematics and reading-comprehension simply by the physical presence of the higher-aptitude pupil. It results in a tension with regard to whose aptitude will be acknowledged and accommodated when designing the course curriculum. The setting or calibration of V^* within a single classroom involves a zero-sum impact between these two pupils. Once again, to avoid this dilemma, these two pupils could be tracked according to present aptitude. However, this is inefficient or costly as argued. Even more to the point, with tracking the pupils are no longer integrated except perhaps at lunch and in extra-curricular activities. So caution should be exercised or the noble pursuit of classroom integration might merely result in lower average achievement, higher costs, and intra-school segregation.

Two additional comments are necessary concerning hypothesis three. The third hypothesis does not follow from the orthodox economic theory of learning where it might be concluded that these integrated, disadvantaged students cause a lower mean q_i/e_i because of alleged "inferior intellectual capacities" stemming from their lower pre-test or lower aptitude scores. The hypothesis follows from scarce instructional targets and differential historical learning, not defective intellectual potential. The theory of instructional error does not deny the presence of legitimate learning handicaps. The theory is concerned with the typical student, not the exception.

Nevertheless, hypothesis three implies that a reckless pursuit of efficiency may encourage a school administrator to adopt the dangerous segregationist mentality of "separate but equal." Because of this, the typical public school is likely to be superior to the typical private school with respect to attaining the third common school goal - integration.

So given this general theory of learning capital, is the public or private sector the most likely candidate to produce the best common school?   Private schools are believed superior in goal one due to *selection efficiency*.   But partly because of this, public schools are likely superior at goal three - integration. Public school enrollment policy is based on residential location and in some places, court-ordered integration. On the other hand, private school enrollment is deliberately based on aptitude homogeneity or *selection efficiency*. So public schools are integrated but less efficient while private schools are segregated but more efficient.

Furthermore, it is uncertain who is superior at equality since public schools are under political mandate to minimize $\Delta\sigma$, while private schools are predicted to minimize $\Delta\sigma$ in order to be *dynamically efficient*. Hence, the theoretical question of whether public or private schools are superior in the simultaneous attainment of the three common school goals is ambiguous.   Empirical analysis provides insight concerning which sector is superior based on the common school criteria.

Notes

1   It might be argued that a teacher should "punish" the pupil(s) neglecting to prepare for a class by moving forward with the curriculum and thus decreasing the learning rate for pupils undisciplined in doing homework consistently. The argument might be that this provides an incentive to prepare for class in the future. However, this belief will not be subscribed to in this analysis even though it is obvious that some type of disciplinary device is necessary to encourage consistent study habits especially in a curriculum that has cumulative pre-requisites.

2   $36,933 is the average annual public-school salary for primary and secondary teachers in the U.S. for school year 1994-1995(from *Digest of Education Statistics*,1995; Table 76, p. 84).

3   This is a permissable simplification since the scores on tests for different cognitive domains are positively correlated for each student. If a pupil is above average in grammar, then it is more likely the student is above average in science

Chapter V

An Empirical Test of the Theory of Learning Capital

This economic analysis of schooling has relied merely on logic and intuition. No empirical data has been offered in support of the central argument that the theory of learning capital is superior to the orthodox economic theory. The objective now is to put the theory of learning capital to the test. In other words, in this chapter hypotheses one and two are empirically tested using multiple regression analysis, while hypothesis three is tested in the next chapter. If hypotheses one and two are supported, then it is believed that the β parameter, introduced in the theory(equation 4.1), is greater than zero and instructional error is an important concept for understanding school efficiency.

Also, given that hypotheses one and two are statistically supported, then a second objective is pursued in this chapter. The public and private schools are ranked according to their attainment of common school goals one and two. In other words, the school sector having the lowest mean value for σ among their respective schools, the better are those schools at attaining *selection efficiency* or maximizing mean q_i/e_i within a school, ceteris paribus. On the other hand, the school sector having the lowest mean value for $\Delta\sigma$ among their respective schools, the better are those schools at attaining both *dynamic efficiency* and equality. Finally, recall that the variables q_i and $\Delta\sigma$ are longitudinal and therefore require time-series data in order to understand and evaluate a school's behavior in its quest to be efficient and equal over time. Using combined cross-sectional and time-series data, the preceding two objectives are now pursued.

5.1 Data Set

The *High School and Beyond* Data is uniquely-suited for testing the theory of learning capital as well as ranking the public and private sectors with respect to efficiency and equality.[1] It is the largest data set ever collected on secondary education in the United States that is both cross-sectional and longitudinal. In the spring of 1980, thirty-six sophomore students were randomly sampled from each of 1,015 schools which were also randomly selected from all regions of the United States. Each student selected was asked to take a battery of seven standardized tests as well as respond to questions regarding family background, study habits, and school experiences. Finally, each school administrator was asked to provide information about their respective schools such as enrollment, staffing patterns, expenditures per-pupil, and special programs.

When these 1980 sophomores were seniors in the spring of 1982 they were asked to take the same cognitive tests over again so as to provide for an unprecedented growth measure over the final two years of high school. School administrators were asked similar questions in 1982 as they were in the base year. Hence, the instructional time period to be empirically analyzed is the final two years of high school for the senior class of 1982. Most important for purposes here is that 86% of the schools in the sample were public while the remaining 14% were private, most of which were Catholic. As discussed previously, this allows for sector comparisons on the basis of comparable data.

The sample is stratified in the sense that some special types of schools were over-sampled so as to test special hypotheses. For example, forty-five of the public schools selected were "alternative" public schools. Eleven of the private, non-Catholic schools selected were "high-performance" schools in the sense that only high-achievers were admitted. Catholic schools with large proportions of Blacks and Cuban/Hispanics were also over-sampled. Due to this stratification and the differential participation rates among students and schools, a weighting scheme is applied to all the analyses in order to make the sample representative of the United States population at the time the sample was drawn. Therefore, average statistics as well as regression parameters are calculated using weighted computations.[2]

In this analyses, the schools will be divided into three sectors: i)public ii)Catholic iii)private, non-Catholic. The participation rate among the schools from the sampling were 91%, 95%, and 76% respectively for each sector. Due to the low participation rate for the private, non-Catholic schools; Coleman, Hoffer, and Greeley(1985), Willms(1985), Alexander and Pallas(1985) and Bryk, Lee, and Holland(1993) excluded them from their analyses. They feared that participation may bias the typical characteristics of these schools in the general population. However, these schools will be retained in this analysis, for they are useful in expanding the range of the experimental variables used to test the *dynamic* and *selection efficiency* hypotheses due to some of the schools being "elite." When making inferences concerning sector performance, these schools are analyzed separately. The reader can judge whether participation might bias the conclusions made about them.

5.2 Regression Model

In order to test for a positive β parameter as expected in equation 4.1, all other influences on school efficiency or achievement growth per-dollar(q_i/e_i) can be controlled using a linear regression model. This regression model and the operational variables used to approximate the theoretical variables are described in table 5.1. The expected sign for the regression parameter corresponding to each independent variable is contained in parenthesis following the definition of each variable. In those cases where a variable is measured by a set of dummy variables, the final category is the residual category and thus has no expected sign. The observations are at the individual student level. Thus, students from the same school have identical values for school-level variables.

Table 5.1
Regression Model for Testing Hypotheses One and Two

Theoretical model(from 4.1):

$$\frac{q_i}{e_i} = \left\{ \frac{\theta_i N}{c + \beta \| V_i - V^* \|} \right\} T_i$$

Functional approximation(5.1):

$\dfrac{q_i}{e_i}$ = f [student, family, community, *c-efficiency, selection efficiency, dynamic efficiency*]

Each category within the functional approximation(5.1) contains a subset of variables selected for the purpose of controlling for the unique effect of the respective category. The two elements of the dependent variable and all the independent variables are categorized, listed, and defined below:

dependent variables.................... q_i, e_i
student variables .... s_1, s_2, s_3, s_4, s_5, s_6
family variables .... f_1, f_2, f_3, f_4, f_5
community variables .... g_1, g_2, g_3, g_4, g_5, g_6, g_7
c-efficiency variables .... c_1, c_2, c_3, c_4, c_5, c_6, c_7, c_8, c_9, c_{10}
selection efficiency variables .... σ, σ^2
dynamic efficiency variables .... $\Delta\sigma$, $\pm [(\Delta\sigma)^2]$

dependent variables:

q_i =	senior composite score(number of items answered correctly: reading comprehension + vocabulary + writing + basic math + advanced math + science + civics) minus sophomore composite score(identical tests) for ith student. Measures cognitive growth over final two years of high school.
e_i =	expenditures per-pupil at the ith student's school over the last two years of high school(capital expenditures are omitted)

Table 5.1 (continued)
Regression Model for Testing Hypotheses One and Two

student:

s_1	=	Sophomore composite test score for ith pupil(?)
s_2	=	Is the ith student handicapped? yes(s_2 = 1) no(s_2 = 0): A student is considered handicapped if the student has at least one of the following conditions as interpreted by the student: a)specific learning disability, b) visual handicap not corrected by glasses, c)hard of hearing, d)deafness, e)speech disability, f)orthopedic handicap, g)other physical disability or handicap(-)
s_3	=	Is the ith student enrolled in the academic track? yes(s_3 = 1) no(s_3 = 0)(+)
s_4	=	Is the ith student enrolled in the vocational track? yes(s_4 = 1) no(s_4 = 0)(-)
s_5	=	Is the ith student enrolled in the general track? (residual category)
s_6	=	Average amount of homework done per-week; measured in hours and interpreted by the student. This is an empirical approximation for time-on-task(T_i)(+)

family:

f_1	=	ith student's parents' socio-economic status. This is a composite variable, traditionally used by educational analysts, comprised of the sum of five standardized and equally weighted variables: 1) father's occupation status as measured by the Duncan SEI scale of occupational categories; 2) father's education; 3) mother's education; 4) family income; 5) the sum of the presence or absence of the following household possessions: daily newspaper, encyclopedia, typewriter, electric dishwasher, >two cars/trucks that run, >50 books, pupil/child's own room, pocket calculator(?)
f_2	=	Does at least one parent expect pupil/child to attend college? yes(f_2 = 1) no(f_2 = 0)(+)
f_3	=	Is the ith student Hispanic? yes(f_3 = 1) no(f_3 = 0)(-)
f_4	=	Is the ith student Black? yes(f_4 = 1) no(f_4 = 0)(-)
f_5	=	Is the ith student neither Hispanic nor Black? (residual category)

Table 5.1 (continued)
Regression Model for Testing Hypotheses One and Two

community:

g_1	=	Is the school that the ith student attends located in an urban area? yes($g_1 = 1$) no($g_1 = 0$)(?)
g_2	=	Is the school that the ith student attends located in a rural area? yes($g_2 = 1$) no($g_2 = 0$)(?)
g_3	=	Is the school that the ith student attends located in a suburban area? (residual category)
g_4	=	Is the school that the ith student attends located in the eastern United States? yes($g_4 = 1$) no($g_4 = 0$)(?)
g_5	=	Is the school that the ith student attends located in the south? yes($g_5 = 1$) no($g_5 = 0$)(?)
g_6	=	Is the school that the ith student attends located in the west? yes($g_6 = 1$) no($g_6 = 0$)(?)
g_7	=	Is the school that the ith student attends located in the northern-middle? (residual category)

c-efficiency:

c_1	=	Proportion of equivalent full-time staff at the ith student's school who are classified as non-classroom teachers(bureaucracy)(-)
c_2	=	Proportion of equivalent full-time staff at the ith student's school who contribute their services free of charge due to being members of religious orders(+)
c_3	=	Proportion of equivalent full-time staff at the ith student's school who are classified as either volunteers or student teachers(+)
c_4	=	Is the ith student attending a school that requires the student to attain a minimum score on a competency test in order to graduate from high school? yes($c_4 = 1$) no($c_4 = 0$)(+)
c_5	=	Are the teachers in the ith student's school represented by a union? yes($c_5 = 1$) no($c_5 = 0$)(?)

Table 5.1 (continued)
Regression Model for Testing Hypotheses One and Two

c_6 = Is the ith student enrolled in a Catholic school? yes(c_6 = 1) no(c_6 = 0)(?)

c_7 = Is the ith student enrolled in a private, non-Catholic school? yes(c_7 = 1) no(c_7 = 0)(?)

c_8 = Is the ith student enrolled in a public school? (residual category)

c_9 = e_i = expenditures per-pupil at the ith student's school over the last two years of high school(capital expenditures are omitted)(same as denominator in dependent variable)(-)

c_{10} = Total high-school enrollment in the ith student's school(defined as N in the theory)(?)

selection efficiency :
_____

σ = standard deviation of sophomore composite test scores for the students in the ith student's school(-)

σ^2 = variance of the sophomore composite test scores for the students in the ith student's school(?)

dynamic efficiency :
_____

$\Delta\sigma$ = standard deviation of senior composite test scores minus the standard deviation of sophomore composite test scores for the students in the ith student's school (i.e. $\Delta\sigma = \sigma_{senior} - \sigma_{sophomore}$)(-)

$\pm [(\Delta\sigma)^2]$ = standard deviation of senior composite test scores minus the standard deviation of sophomore composite test scores *squared* for the students in the ith student's school[i.e. $\pm [(\Delta\sigma)^2] = \pm [(\sigma_{senior} - \sigma_{sophomore})^2]$. The sign of $\Delta\sigma$ is retained for the squared value in order to preserve the direction of the change(?)

In previous estimates of the educational production function, each regression parameter was interpreted as the marginal impact the corresponding independent variable had on q_i since only q_i was the dependent variable. In this analysis however, the parameter measures the relative impact the independent variable has on both q_i and e_i since q_i/e_i is the dependent variable. For example, a variable might increase both q_i and e_i. But if q_i increases more than e_i, the parameter will be positive. On the other hand, if e_i increases proportionately more than q_i, then the parameter will be negative. So both the sign and the relative size of the elasticities between the independent variable and q_i and e_i determines both the size and sign of the corresponding parameter. A more specific explanation for the expected impact of each independent variable is eventually provided.

Keep in mind that the central purpose of the regression model(5.1) is to test hypotheses one and two concerning *selection* and *dynamic efficiency*. Therefore, most of the attention is to be placed on the final four independent variables of the regression model. All of the other explanatory variables are included merely to control for additional causal factors that might influence q_i/e_i. But it does not follow that these other factors are uninteresting or unimportant. The rationale for the inclusion and expected impact of each of these other factors is now offered.

Student. The ith pupil's sophomore composite test score(s_1) is included in the regression in order to control for the ith pupil's previous education, motivation, and industriousness. It is not interpreted as an index for the student's natural rate of learning since this notion, contained within the orthodox theory of learning, has been rejected. Perhaps more important, the sophomore composite test score controls for a possible ceiling-effect on the test. In other words, a student's growth(q_i) may partly depend on the initial starting point(s_1) due to the test questions becoming progressively more difficult or progressively more easy. Or alternatively, the higher a student initially scores, the fewer questions remaining to improve or guess upon. Even though efforts were made to prevent a ceiling-effect when designing the tests, it is impossible to design the perfect test that eliminates any possibility for acceleration or deceleration based solely on the composition of questions. Due to all these potential influences, the sign for the sophomore test score is uncertain(?).

As argued previously, the theory of learning capital does not deny the presence of legitimate mental and physical handicaps. A handicapped condition(s_2) is predicted to lower cognitive growth(q_i) in the numerator due to a student's learning rate(K_i) being lower due to real physical and mental impairments. A handicapped condition might also increase expenditures(e_i) or costs in the denominator due to the school making special arrangements for the ith pupil who is handicapped. The net effect is to decrease q_i/e_i and thus the expected sign for the parameter is negative(-).

Next, being enrolled in the academic track(s_3) and to a lesser extent, the general track(s_5), is expected to have a positive impact on cognitive growth per-dollar relative to enrollment in the vocational track(s_4). The curriculum within the academic track consists mostly of college-preparatory subjects which are also the specific target of the *High School and Beyond* Tests. Contrary to this, a vocational-track curriculum is divided between learning a particular occupational trade such as data-processing or auto-mechanics as well as studying the more traditional, core-curricula of reading, writing, and arithmetic. Nevertheless, it should be noted that instructional error is believed to still have an important influence on efficiency even within the vocational track. Finally, the vocational track is expected to have a larger e_i relative to the academic track due to the vocational track being more equipment intensive. There is likely to be a larger requirement for machines, tools, and materials relative to the academic track. Again, the net effect is for academic-track enrollment to increase q_i/e_i, whereas vocational-track enrollment will lower q_i/e_i.

Finally, the average hours of homework performed per-week(s_6) is an empirical approximation for time-on-task(T_i). Again, this should directly increase q_i while having no impact on e_i and thus the net effect is to increase q_i/e_i. A weakness of this empirical-proxy for time-on-task(T_i) is that it does not measure the intensity of study time. For example, is the homework performed in front of the television or at a quiet desk with minimal distractions? To sum up, all the preceding student variables are included to control for factors influencing q_i/e_i that are peculiar characteristics of the pupil/child and independent of school efficiency.

Family. The second general influence that must be controlled in order to eventually isolate the unique effect a school has on a student's intellectual development is the family influence. In previous studies, the family has been shown to have the largest relative impact on achievement growth(q_i). The family exercises a direct and indirect impact on cognitive growth. First, the parents provide direct learning within the home through conversation, provision of reading material, and perhaps the provision of scholarly activities such as a trip to a museum. So a portion of q_i can be attributed directly to home learning and not school learning. Indirectly, the family either encourages or discourages time-on-task during the formal school day insofar as the parents are a source of encouragement, discipline, guidance, nurturing, and emotional stability. Both of these forces are believed to be present during the final two years of high school. These family influences are difficult to define let alone measure.[3]

Nevertheless, the ith student's parents' socio-economic status(f_1) is included because it has traditionally had a large impact on q_i and has been used frequently by educational analysts to control for the family influences described above. But notice that the expected parameter sign for f_1 is ambiguous or uncertain(?). This is because the parents' socio-economic status(f_1) should be positively related to both q_i and e_i. Therefore, the net effect may be positive, negative, or zero depending on the relative influence. Both the parents' income and their educational attainment, contained within the socio-economic composite variable, increases the demand for learning capital(K_i) for their pupil/child. Thus, the higher the socio-economic status of parents the more committed they are to a higher e_i within their pupil/child's school. For example, higher socio-economic status parents might be willing to tax themselves higher in a public school voting-referendum or pay higher tuition in the private sector since education is an income-elastic service. Both of these possibilities translate into increased expenditures per-pupil(e_i). So it is quite possible for the ith student's parents' socio-economic status, a previously strong explanatory variable for q_i, to have a zero or even a negative net influence on cognitive growth per-dollar(q_i/e_i).

Parents' college expectations for their pupil/child, the second family variable(f_2), accounts for home learning, parents' emotional support, and academic expectations independent of family income and wealth and is therefore expected to be positive($+$).

The final three family variables(f_3 - f_5) account for the effect that race and ethnicity have on educational tastes, family intellectual culture, and the schooling experience unique to minorities. These Black and Hispanic parameters are expected to be negative because being Black or Hispanic has been negatively related to q_i in previous studies.

Community. The final non-efficiency category consists of demographic variables. Variables g_1 through g_3 measure population density as well as the character of the population. The remaining dummy variables(g_4 - g_7) within the community category control for region within the United States. These variables are proxies for numerous factors that vary by geography and in turn influence q_i/e_i. For example, all these community variables control for differential prices encountered for educational inputs. Specifically, average teacher salary is expected to vary with the cost of living between regions as well as the relative attractiveness of a school location within a given region. For example, a salary-premium may be necessary to attract a quality teacher into an urban school where gang violence is prevalent. Also, transportation costs might vary by population density whereas the necessity to heat or cool a school building will vary by climate and thus region. Finally, a high school student's scholastic effort or time-on-task(T_i) might partly depend on the job and college opportunities available in a particular region. Therefore, q_i/e_i may differ depending on the macroeconomic conditions between regions. In conclusion, no a-priori expectations are offered for any of these variables due to all the competing influences.

c-efficiency. All the remaining independent variables are considered school-efficiency variables and are therefore the responsibility of school administrators and teachers. The rationale for the influence of most of these variables was provided in the previous chapter. Again, for the *c-efficiency variables*, the expected impact depends on whether the school input adds more to expenditures($eN\theta_i$) or output(K^*) in the ith student's respective track. This indirectly determines whether c increases or decreases within the denominator of the theoretical model for q_i/e_i(4.1).

Variable c_1 is the proportion of staff classified as non-classroom teachers. It is presumed that these non-teaching, support personnel contribute more to costs($eN\theta_i$) than to output(K^*) and thus the variable is expected to lower q_i/e_i. Next, variables c_2 and c_3 measure the extent to which the school enjoys donated labor from members of religious orders, student teachers, and volunteers. These positions are expected to produce a higher K^* at no additional cost and therefore the net effect is to decrease c which increases q_i/e_i.

Variable c_4, the requirement for passing a graduation test, was included for several reasons. First, this school policy is expected to raise the intensity of the student's study-time(T_i) as well as discourage grade inflation by having an objective measure of educational attainment. Second, it controls for the presence or absence of a large bloc of time-on-task(T_i) coming at the end of the senior year in order to review and cram for this graduation examination. This potential bloc of time-on-task(T_i) is likely to be omitted from average hours of homework per-week measured previously by student-variable six(s_6). Third, the graduation-test variable controls for any test-taking skills a pupil might acquire by being more familiar and comfortable with standardized tests. Finally, variable c_4 is a previously ignored, policy-relevant variable since politicians have recommended the implementation of a national test for the purpose of monitoring and encouraging academic performance. No doubt, there is likely to be some administrative costs in implementing the test, but these costs are probably minor in comparison to the increase in q_i stemming from more time-on-task(T_i). Hence, the net effect of having a minimum competency test is predicted to increase q_i/e_i.

The next *c-efficiency* variable is a dummy variable(c_5) that equals one if the teachers at the ith pupil's school are represented by a union. Out of the schools that were organized, most teachers were represented by either the *National Education Association* or the *American Federation of Teachers*. The ith pupil's teachers being unionized is likely to have two effects. First, unions encourage and finance professional teacher development and therefore teacher productivity through direct research on pedagogy and the dissemination of this research through teacher workshops. The union also provides a single voice for teachers to petition school administrators to implement policies that are mutually-beneficial for all interested parties. This part of union behavior should increase K* and thus increase q_i. The union also represents the salary interests of teachers which indirectly raises costs or e_i. Therefore, no commitment is made on the net effect a union has on c and therefore school efficiency(q_i/e_i).

Finally, the school sector dummy variables(c_6 - c_8) are included in the *c-efficiency* category to control for unrecognized and omitted factors that vary across sectors. No evaluation is to be made concerning sector quality using these parameters because the variables merely account for residual variation remaining across sectors. Most important, the inclusion of these sector dummy-variables eliminates the selection-bias critique for comparing public and private-school quality. For purposes here, if there is to be a sector advantage, it will be traced to the specific school policies of *selection* and *dynamic efficiency*.

To conclude, variables $e_i(c_9)$ and $N(c_{10})$ are included to control for diminishing returns to funding(e_i) and school enrollment(N) as discussed in the previous chapter.

Selection and Dynamic Efficiency. Finally and most important, if the regression parameter for the variable σ, under *selection efficiency*, is negative and statistically significant, then hypothesis number one is supported. Similarly, if the parameter for variable $\Delta\sigma$, under *dynamic efficiency*, is negative and statistically significant, then hypothesis two is supported. The second variable within both of these respective efficiency categories tests for a potential non-linear relationship between aptitude dispersion and efficiency both at the beginning of the instructional period and over time. Taken together, these parameters test whether β is positive and/or large on the margin; and thus, whether the theoretical discussion of learning capital was valid. Finally, notice that the expected parameter signs for the variables σ and $\Delta\sigma$ are unambiguous. A larger dispersion of aptitudes in the present(σ) and over time($\Delta\sigma$) is expected to lower the numerator(q_i) and/or increase the denominator(e_i).[4]

A more detailed discussion is necessary concerning what is being measured with these *selection* and *dynamic efficiency* variables. To begin, the dispersion of aptitudes(σ) and the change in the dispersion of aptitudes($\Delta\sigma$) are neither a direct measure for instructional error nor a direct measure for the change in instructional error. It is possible to have large instructional error and zero aptitude dispersion if the instructional target is pareto inferior. It is also possible to have zero instructional error within a school while also having a large dispersion of aptitudes if an expensive tutorial is implemented in a school. To measure instructional error directly, both the instructional target within the ith pupil's aptitude track(V^*) as well as the aptitude of the ith pupil(V_i) would both have to be known. Obtaining these measures would be difficult even if a skilled observer monitored every classroom in every school over the two-year period of the study.

Given this difficulty in directly measuring instructional error, what is the standard deviation of aptitudes within a school measuring? The dispersion of aptitudes is merely an indicator for how costly it is to minimize instructional error and thus provide a maximum average learning rate for a student body given that the instructional target($V*$) is pareto optimal. Even with a pareto optimal $V*$, a large dispersion of aptitudes forces the school to operate either with a few aptitude tracks that have large amounts of instructional error or make the necessary expenditures in offering many tracks with unique and pareto-optimal $V*$'s. No matter which of these two policies a school adopts, the expected level for q_i/e_i decreases the larger the values for σ and $\Delta\sigma$ even when the $V*$'s are pareto-optimal.

An additional measurement problem arises if $V*$ is pareto inferior. The *c-efficiency* variables must be relied upon to account for these inflated instructional-error inefficiencies that arise even when σ and $\Delta\sigma$ remain constant while $V*$ becomes sub-optimal. So the dispersion of aptitudes measures the cost of reducing aggregate instructional error under the most ideal situation where $V*$ is at least pareto optimal. From this, it can be concluded that the dispersion of aptitudes measures the minimum impact instructional error has on school efficiency(q_i/e_i).

Finally, even though a direct measure for $V*$ is unavailable, it does not follow that the location of a school's average instructional target($V*$) is completely unknown. The *dynamic efficiency* variable, $\Delta\sigma = \sigma_{senior} - \sigma_{sophomore}$, for a school contains some information concerning the location of $V*$ within the school. Again, $\Delta\sigma$ measures the change in the dispersion of aptitudes for the ith pupil's school peers during the final two years of high school. It is the most direct measure for how committed a school is to equality of opportunity and the corresponding result - equality of outcomes. Thus, it is used as a direct measure for the extent a school accomplishes the second common school goal - equality of opportunity. It is a more demanding measure in that it measures equality of outcomes rather than equality of opportunity. It measure success rather than effort.

Using this equality measure and the theory of learning capital, the following inference can be made: The lower a school's value for $\Delta\sigma$, the lower is $V*$ relative to the pupils' aptitudes(V_i). Or alternatively, the higher a school's value for $\Delta\sigma$, the higher is $V*$ relative to the pupils' aptitudes($V*$). In summary, the lower $\Delta\sigma$ for a particular school, the more that school is concentrating resources on the lower-aptitude students relative to higher-aptitude students over time. Also notice that $\Delta\sigma$ can range from negative to positive infinity, and once again, the lower $\Delta\sigma$ the more equal is the school. To conclude, σ and $\Delta\sigma$ are reasonably good variables to both measure the opportunity costs of having instructional error or the opportunity costs of minimizing instructional error as well as measuring school equality.

Strangely enough, the previous analysts of the *High School and Beyond* Data did not report the value for $\Delta\sigma$ for the typical school within each sector(Coleman, Hoffer, and Greeley, 1985; Willms, 1985; Alexander and Pallas, 1985; Chubb and Moe, 1990; Bryk, Lee, and Holland, 1993). It is strange because concern for equality is prevalent throughout their analyses. This suggests that the theoretical model guiding their empirical analyses is too static. In addition, the average value for σ among the schools within each sector also goes unreported in previous analyses. This is further evidence that *instructional error* and its effect on efficiency did not guide the empirical specification of their theoretical models. Again, part of the reason why aptitude-dispersion measures have been ignored is theoretical. The pupils' learning rates have been considered exogenous parameters to be either enjoyed or tolerated, not endogenous variables to be maximized.

The inclusion of the *dynamic* and *selection efficiency* variables is not the only manner in which this regression differs from the previous regressions performed on the *High School and Beyond* Data. Again, Coleman, Hoffer, and Greeley(1985); Willms(1985); Alexander and Pallas(1985); Chubb and Moe(1990); and Bryk, Lee, and Holland(1993) use q_i as their dependent variable. These analysts simply ignore e_i except for Chubb and Moe(1990) and Bryk, Lee, and Holland(1993) who included it as an independent variable.[5]

However, q_i/e_i is a superior dependent variable for several reasons.[6] First, without including e_i in the dependent variable, it is impossible to capture the behavior of schools spending themselves out of the high aptitude-dispersion problem simply by providing more costly tracks. The objective should be to measure the opportunity costs of aptitude dispersion which can be in the form of a lower q_i, or higher e_i, or both. Second, this dependent variable allows for a more direct policy interpretation. School sectors can be distinguished by who produces the most growth(q_i) if each sector spent the same amount of money. If a government had e_i to spend for a student and just wanted to maximize q_i for the student, then the government would allocate the resources(e_i) and the student toward the sector having the largest K_i/e_i or q_i/e_i ratio on the margin. Third, this specification permits a direct test of element two of the orthodox economic theory of learning. In other words, does there really exist a tradeoff between efficiency(q_i/e_i) and equality($\Delta\sigma$)? Or alternatively, are efficiency and equality complementary goals as hypothesized here. Finally, this overall regression model is believed to be an improvement since it measures the effect each factor has on a school's ability to get the most from its given resources; not which school or sector can obtain the most resources.

5.3   *Weaknesses of the Data*

Before reporting the mean values for the variables as well as the regression results, it is important to acknowledge the weaknesses of the *High School and Beyond* Data and discuss the adjustments made to overcome problems. The first problem concerns the definition of e_i. School administrators were asked to supply both high school and district expenditures per-pupil for each of the final two years of high school for the senior class of 1982. District expenditures per-pupil is the sum of: district-wide administrative expenditures per-pupil, elementary and middle-school expenditures per-pupil, and high school expenditures per-pupil. High school expenditures per-pupil includes only expenditures made within the high school. On the average, district expenditures per-pupil are *smaller* than high school expenditures per-pupil because the much lower elementary and middle-school expenditures per-pupil pulls the district average below the high school average even with district-wide administrative expenditures included.

The problem is that some schools reported only one or the other. Relatively more public schools reported district expenditures rather than high school expenditures simply because public schools are managed at the district level and private high schools exist independently. Thus, direct comparison is problematic. Given this, e_i is defined as follows:

e_i = junior year expenditures per-pupil + senior year expenditures per-pupil

where:

expenditures per-pupil in the respective year =

1) high school expenditures per-pupil if it is reported for the given year.
2) if high school expenditures are un-reported for a given year but district expenditures are reported, then district expenditures are used as a proxy for high school expenditures per-pupil.
3) if neither high school nor district expenditures are reported for a given year but at least one is reported for the other year, then the other year's expenditures are used to approximate the expenditures missing in the given year(negligible subset).
4) if neither high school nor district expenditures per-pupil were reported in any year, the students in the school were eliminated from the analysis(negligible subset).

High school expenditures per-pupil are theoretically correct since only high school students are being analyzed, not elementary and middle-school students. This is why high-school expenditures are always used if available. This definition biases e_i for a public school downward since relatively more of their high school expenditures are approximated by the lower district expenditures per-pupil. However, with the inclusion of the sector dummy variables(c_6 - c_8) and $e_i(c_9)$ as controls in the regression model, much of this bias is controlled.

Nevertheless, testing for the existence of *selection* and *dynamic efficiency* is still possible even with public school expenditures per-pupil(e_i) under-estimated and their corresponding efficiency ratio(q_i/e_i) over-estimated. In fact, the definition for e_i biases the parameters for σ and $\Delta\sigma$ from their hypothesized negative values toward zero or the null hypothesis. This is because public schools have relatively larger values for σ and $\Delta\sigma$ as will be shown. In other words, public schools will have an artificially high q_i/e_i while also having relatively larger values for σ and $\Delta\sigma$, which is counter to the expectations derived from theory. So the definition for e_i makes for a more conservative testing of hypotheses one and two since the definition slants the empirical test toward the rejection of hypotheses one and two.

Besides these problems associated with e_i, four additional adjustments are made. Over the two-year time span of the study, some of the students who participated in the base year test and survey were not present in their school during the follow-up test and survey. A relatively small proportion of the students either graduated early, dropped out of high school, or transferred to another high school. A subset of these students were contacted for a follow-up test and survey. However, following the lead of the previous analysts(Coleman, Hoffer, and Greeley,1985; Willms,1985; Alexander and Pallas,1985; Chubb and Moe, 1990; Bryk, Lee, and Holland 1993), only those students still attending their base year school at the end of their senior year are included. The possible bias this introduces is discussed within the next section of this chapter. In regression number three it is shown that the exclusion of these students does not significantly alter the estimated parameters for *selection* and *dynamic efficiency*.

Second, given the definition of e_i, the expenditure levels that some school administrators reported were too low. In other words, it was fiscally impossible to meet the school's payroll given their reported salary and staffing patterns while spending the amount they claimed. Less than one percent of the observations were purged by eliminating students attending schools with $e_i < \$50$. The elimination was roughly proportional across sectors. The only justification needed for this adjustment is that the school surveys were internally inconsistent and therefore useless.

Third, in order to increase the number of observations suitable for the regression by 9%, a few of the missing independent variables were estimated using the school sector(public; Catholic; private, non-Catholic) mean value. No test scores were ever estimated and only the missing values for "minor" variables were estimated.[7] It is shown in regression number five that this adjustment has no impact on the qualitative conclusions concerning *selection* and *dynamic efficiency*.

Finally, the test scores used are the raw number of correct items as used by Coleman, Hoffer, and Greeley(1985) and Alexander and Pallas(1985). However, Willms(1985) and Chubb and Moe(1990) recommend using formula test scores that are adjusted for guessing. It is shown in regression number four that the estimated parameters for *selection* and *dynamic efficiency* are relatively insensitive to whether raw or formula scores are used.

5.4 *Bias Toward the Null Hypotheses*

In summary, it is believed that the adjustments made on the data makes for a more conservative test for both hypothesis one and two. There are several reasons for this conclusion. First, as discussed previously, the definition of e_i biases the efficiency ratio upward for public schools who also have the largest values for σ and $\Delta\sigma$. Thus, the parameters for these variables are biased toward zero. This bias is exacerbated since each high school's share of public school administrative expenditures at all levels above the school district(city, county, state, Federal) are omitted.[8]

Second, part of the reason a student may graduate early, drop out, or transfer to another school is due to that student suffering from high instructional error. A dropout may be in the lower tail of the aptitude distribution; whereas an early graduate may be in the upper tail. A transfer could be in either tail. Being in these extreme positions lowers the possibility of having an optimal instructional target and thus enjoying any significant rate of learning. As a result, the student leaves the school. By omitting these students from the analysis, σ and $\Delta\sigma$ are underestimated for all schools.

Finally, the instructional error the ith student experiences($\|V_i - V^*\|$) is expected to partially influence the following: time-on-task(T_i measured by s_6), track assignment($s_3 - s_5$), parents' expectations(f_2), % of staff that are remedial specialists(within variable c_1), and perhaps whether a student defines himself as having a learning handicap(s_2). However, in the regression model(5.1), all these independent variables are controlled. Thus, the effect of instructional error is perhaps, again, underestimated since instructional error would indirectly lower q_i/e_i through the indirect alteration of these other independent variables. To sum up, since these adjustments bias the parameter estimates for σ and $\Delta\sigma$ from their hypothesized negative values toward zero, the estimates should be interpreted as a lower-bound estimate on the effect aptitude dispersion has on the expected q_i/e_i within a school.

Table 5.2 lists the mean values by sector for the dependent and independent variables used in the regression model(5.1). Recall that the mean values in table 5.2 are weighted and therefore representative of the student and school population at the time the sample was drawn. Of course, the median values listed for σ and $\Delta\sigma$ are not weighted.

Table 5.2
Mean Values for Regression Variables by Sector

variable	public	Catholic	private, non-Catholic
cognitive achievement growth (q_i)	7.29	9.19	8.76
expenditures per-pupil (e_i)(c_9)	$3579.31	$2446.74	$4864.71
efficiency ratio or dependent variable = (q_i/e_i)x(10,000)	27.56	40.59	22.65
sophomore test score (s_1)	67.94	76.58	79.15
handicap status (s_2)	.2373	.2402	.2858
academic track (s_3)	.3407	.6137	.6186
vocational track (s_4)	.1955	.0583	.0508
time-on-task (T_i)(s_6)	4.603	5.252	5.414
parents' socio-economic status (f_1)	-26.243	334.255	545.94
parents' college expectations (f_2)	.6647	.8498	.7772
Hispanic student (f_3)	.1204	.0863	.0530
Black student (f_4)	.1043	.0351	.0246
urban school (g_1)	.1604	.1287	.2414
rural school (g_2)	.3783	.1612	.3194
% of staff that are non-teachers (c_1)	.1789	.1766	.1864
% religious contributed services (c_2)	.0116	.0976	0.00
% volunteers + student teachers (c_3)	.0537	.0603	.0982
test for graduation (c_4)	.2224	.1322	.0821
teachers unionized (c_5)	.8434	.1975	0.00
Catholic school (c_6)	0.00	0.113	0.00
private, non-Catholic school (c_7)	0.00	0.00	0.032
high school enrollment (N)(c_{10})	1258.53	833.03	593.65
σ mean	18.6547	16.482	16.856
(median)	(18.7904)	(16.733)	(12.506)
$\Delta\sigma$ mean	1.31	0.6215	0.401
(median)	(1.31)	(0.9675)	(-0.5435)

Notice that both private sectors have a lower value for σ, on the average, as expected. So the typical student body is eleven percent more homogeneous in the private sector compared to the public sector at the beginning of the instructional period. Whether this is significant depends on how sensitive q_i/e_i is to σ.

5.5 Who Produces More Equality?

The most surprising averages appear in the last row for $\Delta\sigma$. To find equal values for $\Delta\sigma$ across the sectors would be surprising given the orthodox economic theory of learning. For the primary rationale for public provision of primary and secondary education is to insure more equality or a lower $\Delta\sigma$ than is expected to be forthcoming from the private sector. But these averages go further. They demonstrate that the typical private school produces more equality than the typical public school. Or similarly, the private sector is superior at minimizing the growth of inequality over the two-year instructional period. The typical or mean private, non-Catholic school is 69% more equal than the mean public school; while the mean Catholic school is 53% more equal. The median private, non-Catholic school actually produces more equality, rather than merely minimizing the growth of inequality, and is thus 142% more equal than the mean public school. So it would seem that the market incentive to be equitable is stronger and more effective than political decree. Or comparatively speaking, in a politically managed school the higher aptitude pupil/families are able to hold θ_i and V^* hostage and thus impose the costs of having a large σ on their lower-aptitude colleagues.

However, these findings should be viewed as preliminary because the private sector's ability to produce this equality advantage may stem from the peculiarities of each sector's average student body characteristics, especially with respect to the diversity or integration attained. For it may be easier to produce equality for a more culturally homogeneous group of students. But for now, the sectors can be ordered as follows with respect to attaining the second common school goal of equality of opportunity: 1)private, non-Catholic 2)Catholic 3)public. The next question is whether smaller values for $\Delta\sigma$ as well as σ leads to higher expected values for q_i/e_i and thus whether the typical private school is both more equal and more efficient.

5.6 *Regression Results*

The estimated parameters for the regression model(5.1) are listed in table 5.3. Regression number one is the primary regression to focus upon from which conclusions will be drawn. Regressions two through five test for parameter sensitivity to alternative specifications. The t-statistic for each parameter is in parenthesis directly below the estimated parameter. The p-values for each parameter is denoted by an asterisk(s). A p-value of less than or equal to .05, .001, or .0001 corresponds to one, two, or three asterisks, respectively. All p-values are for a two-tailed test.

Before discussing whether the hypotheses one and two were supported, some 'non-instructional error' results are discussed. First, notice that a student's sophomore test score(s_i) is negatively related to q_i/e_i across all the regressions. Hence, the higher the student's initial achievement the *lower* his learning rate(K_i) or cognitive growth(q_i) over the final two years of high school. This contradicts element one of the orthodox economic theory of learning. This should not be alarming since we had no a-priori expectations for this relationship given the rejection of the natural-aptitude or natural learning rate philosophy. The best explanation for this is that a ceiling-effect exists on the test despite efforts to minimize it.

It might be argued that this empirical result is contradictory to Chubb and Moe's(1990) finding on the same data. For they found a positive parameter for sophomore test scores(s_i) when using q_i as their dependent variable. But it must be recognized that they used "log gain scores" as the dependent variable rather than mere gain scores(q_i). This has the effect of weighting a student's q_i more the larger their sophomore score. This in turn has the effect of inflating the parameter for the sophomore composite test score. Chubb and Moe(1990, p. 76) reasoned that this should be done in order to control for the initially low-achiever regressing to the mean when taking the senior test. However, this is not persuasive because a student scoring high on the sophomore test will also regress downward toward the mean on the senior test. Hence, no persuasive reason remains for using "log gain scores."

For the most part, the a-priori predictions for the other parameter signs were borne out. There is one significant exception. The measure for bureaucracy(c_i) *within* a high school was predicted to have a

Table 5.3
Regression Results for Dependent Variable q_i/e_i

regression 1: basic model; **regression 2:** aptitude dispersion measures omitted; **regression 3:** early graduates and dropouts included; **regression 4:** formula test scores adjusted for guessing are used rather than raw test scores; **regression 5:** missing values for $s_6(T_i)$, $c_{10}(N)$, and parents' socio-economic status (f_1) are not estimated using sector means as they are in regression one.

variable	1	2	3	4	5
intercept	272.350*** (17.273)	86.683*** (15.007)	240.081*** (16.355)	286.978*** (14.602)	295.982*** (16.537)
sophomore composite test score (s_1)	-0.4462*** (-9.478)	-0.4872*** (-10.285)	-0.4409*** (-9.548)	-0.4366*** (-9.651)	-0.4565*** (-8.902)
student's self-described handicap status (s_2)	-2.5314 (-1.416)	-02.3134 (-1.285)	-3.1670 (-1.809)	-3.2086 (-1.456)	-2.5821 (-1.334)
academic track (s_3)	4.9345* (2.614)	5.8919* (3.097)	5.1664* (2.793)	5.6709* (2.435)	4.8806* (2.393)
vocational track (s_4)	-6.9526* (3.219)	-6.9183* (-3.178)	-5.8880* (-2.797)	-8.5877* (-3.223)	-7.1491* (-3.002)
time-on-task (T_i)(s_6)	1.8357* (2.896)	1.9175* (2.999)	1.6879* (2.725)	2.3459* (2.999)	1.5826* (2.292)
parents' socio-economic status (f_1)	-0.0004 (-0.313)	-0.00008 (-0.060)	-0.00006 (-0.048)	0.00 (0.00)	-0.0001 (-0.095)
parents' college expectations (f_2)	8.9536*** (4.876)	8.9358*** (4.829)	8.4841*** (4.736)	11.2300*** (4.962)	9.4893*** (4.702)
Hispanic student (f_3)	-7.75* (-3.043)	-6.19* (-2.413)	-6.8491* (-2.757)	-9.0151* (-2.870)	-6.7948* (-2.423)
Black student (f_4)	-18.511*** (-6.317)	-15.467*** (-5.258)	-17.4679*** (-6.083)	-22.1788*** (-6.147)	-19.3396*** (-5.844)
urban school (g_1)	1.7413 (0.751)	4.5762* (1.968)	2.3185 (1.029)	3.0935 (1.083)	3.0560 (1.198)
rural school (g_2)	-4.606* (-2.467)	-5.528* (-2.948)	-4.6130* (-2.515)	-6.4063* (-2.784)	-3.8526 (-1.895)
east (g_4)	10.041*** (4.343)	12.743*** (5.490)	11.6387*** (5.123)	14.2646*** (5.002)	10.7729*** (4.265)
south (g_5)	-6.015* (-2.67)	-4.843* (-2.147)	-6.7324* (-3.057)	-7.1179* (-2.561)	-7.0727* (-2.873)
west (g_6)	8.793*** (3.871)	11.136*** (4.875)	8.6687*** (3.906)	10.9249*** (3.904)	8.5066** (3.475)

*p-value ≤ .05   **p-value ≤ .001   ***p-value ≤ .0001
all p-values for two-tailed test

(continued)

Learning Capital

Table 5.3 (continued)
Regression Results for Dependent Variable q_i/e_i

regression 1: basic model; regression 2: aptitude dispersion measures omitted; regression 3: early graduates and dropouts included; regression 4: formula test scores adjusted for guessing are used rather than raw test scores; regression 5: missing values for $s_6(T_i)$, $c_{10}(N)$, and parents' socio-economic status (f_1) are not estimated using sector means as they are in regression one.

variable	1	2	3	4	5
% of staff: non-classroom teachers (c_1)	65.7148*** (6.558)	81.3151*** (8.111)	80.1818*** (8.233)	86.1138*** (6.963)	81.7849*** (6.975)
% of staff: religious contributed services (c_2)	3.633 (0.361)	7.7459 (0.766)	8.7450 (0.902)	10.5806 (0.854)	-0.0183 (-0.002)
% of staff: volunteers + student teachers (c_3)	-1.119 (-0.123)	1.577 (0.172)	-4.4605 (-0.504)	-0.6981 (-.062)	3.2739 (0.335)
graduation test (c_4)	5.418* (2.731)	5.854* (2.928)	6.0753* (3.138)	6.1036* (2.494)	5.9334* (2.732)
teachers unionized (c_5)	-1.001 (-0.436)	-0.4453 (-0.193)	-1.3137 (-0.583)	-1.4470 (-0.512)	-2.8416 (-1.104)
Catholic School (c_6)	-11.38* (-3.055)	-10.893* (-2.934)	-11.428* (-3.090)	-15.4877** (-3.369)	-12.580* (-3.102)
private, non-Catholic school (c_7)	8.059 (1.593)	13.633* (2.686)	11.1425* (2.221)	10.4952 (1.681)	5.8123 (1.084)
expenditures per-pupil (e_i)(c_9)	-0.0167*** (-26.826)	-0.016*** (-25.534)	-0.0167*** (-27.426)	-0.0208*** (-27.049)	-0.0175*** (-25.991)
high school enrollment (N)(c_{10})	-.0005 (-.037)	0.0008 (0.603)	-0.0004 (-0.319)	0.0004 (0.280)	-0.0006 (-0.422)
σ	-19.6280*** (-12.505)	---	-16.6270*** (-11.499)	-15.8728*** (-10.360)	-22.0391*** (-12.243)
σ^2	0.5246*** (12.150)	---	0.4518*** (11.350)	0.3294*** (10.037)	0.5947*** (11.908)
$\Delta\sigma$	-5.7234*** (-7.620)	---	-4.7385*** (-6.496)	-3.1264*** (-4.206)	-7.3763*** (-8.655)
$\pm [(\Delta\sigma)^2]$	1.3679*** (8.896)	---	1.0619*** (7.188)	0.5113*** (4.213)	1.7970*** (10.012)
adjusted R^2	.0714	.0556	.0715	.0655	.0763
n = student observations	15,714	15,714	16,081	15,714	14,251
F-statistic	45.753	41.186	46.874	41.759	44.571

*p-value $\leq$ .05   **p-value $\leq$ .001   ***p-value $\leq$ .0001
all p-values for two-tailed test

negative impact on efficiency. It had a large and positive effect. Probing the definition for this variable in more detail provides insight:

% of equivalent full-time staff who are non-classroom teachers(c_1) =

[assistant principals and deans + counselors + curriculum specialists + remedial specialists + library/media personnel + psychologists + teacher aides + security guards] / [numerator + classroom teachers]

The impact of each individual staff position as a percentage of the entire staff was analyzed by running separate regressions(unreported here). The efficiency-enhancing positions are listed in descending order of their positive and statistically significant impact: 1)security guards 2)psychologists 3)teacher aides 4)counselors 5)remedial specialists. The impact of each remaining staff position was either significantly negative or statistically insignificant.

So why do some bureaucratic positions improve efficiency? Casual conversation with teachers leads to the following two explanations for why some of these bureaucratic positions were significant in raising q_i/e_i. First, with these staff available, a teacher is able to turn a disruptive student over to them. This allows the teacher to concentrate on the management of learning and not on the management of learners during valuable class time. It is perhaps sad that an optimal policy to stimulate intellectual growth is to convert the school librarian into the school cop. Second, with teacher aides available, a teacher is likely to assign more homework that will also be more thoroughly graded by aides. And some of these aides are less expensive than teachers since many are not college graduates or certified in teaching.

Most important, the parameters for σ and $\Delta\sigma$ have the expected signs and are statistically significant. Yet, there is also a statistically-significant, non-linear effect on q_i/e_i with respect to aptitude dispersion. So the sign and magnitude of the relationship depends on the initial values for σ and $\Delta\sigma$. Also, even though the size of the parameters for the *selection* and *dynamic efficiency* variables change somewhat across regressions one through five, the sign and level of statistical significance for each aptitude dispersion measure is insensitive to whether: i) early graduates and dropouts are included(regression 3), ii) test scores are adjusted for guessing(regression 4), or whether iii) the sample size is reduced due to the "minor" missing variables not being estimated(regression 5). There is no instance in which a p-value falls above .0001 for any of these parameters. Hence, even with this conservative test where the parameters were believed to be biased toward zero, the parameters are robust and significantly different from zero.

Further notice how the adjusted R^2 decreases from regression one to regression two when only the *selection* and *dynamic efficiency* variables are deleted.[9] The R^2 falls 22.1%. This is significant since only four variables measuring essentially the same thing are deleted from the original twenty-four. Also, when these aptitude-dispersion measures are deleted from regression one, it alters the parameters for the school sector dummy variables rather significantly. The unexplained private, non-Catholic efficiency advantage over the public sector increases 69% and becomes statistically significant. The residual or unexplained Catholic-public differential is reduced by only 4%. Together, this is preliminary evidence that there is at least some private-school advantage in minimizing σ and $\Delta\sigma$ and thus achieving higher *selection* and *dynamic efficiency*.

Finally, there is some concern in using $e_i(c_9)$ as an independent variable to control for diminishing returns to funding since it is part of the dependent variable(q_i/e_i). Regression number six, presented in table 5.4, is offered to show that the aptitude dispersion parameters are not disturbed when e_i is replaced by four independent variables that measure educational inputs or the composition of expenditures per-pupil(e_i) in more detail. These educational inputs are: 1) average teacher quality(starting teacher salary), 2) teachers' education or academic competence(% of teachers with advanced degrees), 3) teachers' experience(% of teachers at school more than ten years), and 4) average class size(N/classroom teachers).

So disaggregating e_i lowers the adjusted R^2 by 36.5% and eliminates the statistical significance for the graduation test and the regional dummy variables. It also reverses the signs of the school sector dummy variables. It is interesting to note that a school can improve efficiency(q_i/e_i) by concentrating relatively more resources on the retention of experienced teachers rather than offer higher starting salaries or larger salary increments for graduate degrees. This result concerning teacher longevity is inconsistent with the notion of the lazy, tenured teacher. Finally, this positive result for teacher

Table 5.4
Regression Result for Dependent Variable q_i/e_i

regression 6: e_i disagreggated into detailed expenditure items

variable	6
intercept	289.620***
	(16.931)
sophomore composite test score (s_1)	-0.4858***
	(-10.182)
student's self-described handicap status (s_2)	-2.0755
	(-1.145)
academic track (s_3)	4.3288*
	(2.261)
vocational track (s_4)	-7.6340**
	(-3.484)
time-on-task (T_i)(s_6)	1.5284*
	(2.378)
parents' socio-economic status (f_1)	-0.0019
	(-1.459)
parents' college expectations (f_2)	9.3624***
	(5.028)
Hispanic student (f_3)	-8.7315**
	(-3.380)
Black student (f_4)	-22.628***
	(-7.614)
urban school (g_1)	5.6033*
	(2.380)
rural school (g_2)	-4.4595*
	(-2.330)
east (g_4)	-4.1633
	(-1.753)
south (g_5)	-0.2949
	(-0.126)
west (g_6)	3.5925
	(1.540)

*p-value $\leq$ .05   **p-value $\leq$ .001   ***p-value $\leq$ .0001
all p-values for two-tailed test

(continued)

Table 5.4 (continued)
Regression Result for Dependent Variable q_i/e_i

regression 6: e_i disagreggated into detailed expenditure items

variable	6
% of staff: non-classroom teachers (c_1)	40.1874** (3.641)
% of staff: religious + contributed services (c_2)	16.5784 (1.625)
% of staff: volunteers + student teachers (c_3)	-11.5959 (-1.234)
graduation test (c_4)	2.407 (1.199)
teachers unionized (c_5)	-0.7917 (-0.338)
Catholic School (c_6)	0.9317 (0.240)
private, non-Catholic school (c_7)	-16.048* (-3.127)
expenditures per-pupil (e_i)(c_9)	---
starting teacher salary for bachelors degree	-0.009835*** (-14.782)
% of teachers at school with masters or Ph.D.	-0.1249* (-3.155)
% of teachers at school greater than ten years	0.2654*** (6.674)
class size = N/classroom teachers	0.0071 (0.691)
high school enrollment (N)	0.0038* (2.843)
σ	-16.8770*** (-10.555)
σ^2	0.4578*** (10.409)
$\Delta\sigma$	-4.8729*** (-6.393)
$\pm [(\Delta\sigma)^2]$	1.2857*** (8.242)
adjusted R^2	0.0453
n=student observations	15,714
F-statistic	25.843

*p-value ≤ .05   **p-value ≤ .001   ***p-value ≤ .0001
all p-values for two-tailed test

experience is consistent with past production-function research(Hanushek; 1986, 1989).

But the important thing to note in regression six is that the parameters for aptitude dispersion are once again relatively unaltered by disaggregating e_i. Also, the effect of aptitude dispersion is unaffected even when controlling for a school's average class size. This supports the earlier argument that dividing students into smaller groups does not efficiently overcome the problem of high aptitude dispersion because this spreads the school's budget too thinly.

Before analyzing whether the instructional-error hypotheses were supported, some comments are necessary concerning the parameter signs of the sector dummy variables under the *c-efficiency* category. Recall that the rationale for their inclusion is to differentiate clearly the effect of aptitude dispersion and any undetected and unmeasured influences that might vary by sector such as persistent pareto-inferior instructional targets(V^*). They were also included to eliminate any remaining selection bias not controlled by the student and family variables. Notice in regression one the Catholic sector parameter is significantly negative while the private, non-Catholic sector is positive but statistically insignificant. Also notice that in regression six the precise opposite results are obtained: the Catholic sector parameter is positive but insignificant while the private, non-Catholic parameter is negative and statistically significant.

The first conclusion that might be drawn from these two regression results is that on the average the unexplained variation in q_i/e_i does not consistently vary by sector. In other words, any selection bias that might exist has been eliminated and the public, Catholic, and private, non-Catholic sectors are roughly equal in remaining variation. So any potential differential in sector performance can be traced to the independent variables already present in the general model.

There is perhaps a better explanation for the sector parameter signs in regressions one and six. The crucial difference between regressions one and six is that regression one includes e_i as an independent variable while e_i is omitted in regression six. The omission of e_i seriously undermines the explanatory power of regression one since R^2 decreases by 37% even when four educational inputs are substituted for e_i. The question that must be answered is why a sign reversal occurs between regressions one and six for the sector parameters when e_i is omitted.

To address this question, regression one can be represented by line one in figure 5.1. It illustrates the idea of diminishing returns to funding. In other words, q_i/e_i decreases as e_i increases. The slope of this line is largely determined by the public schools since they account for 85% of the observations. Notice that the public schools are concentrated at average values for both q_i/e_i and e_i which is appropriate given the average statistics in table 5.2. The Catholic sector dummy variable has a negative parameter in regression one because the Catholic schools are concentrated below line one in figure 5.1 as illustrated. The private, non-Catholic parameter is positive in regression one because those schools are concentrated above line one as illustrated. So with the independent variable e_i included in regression one, the sector parameter signs make sense.

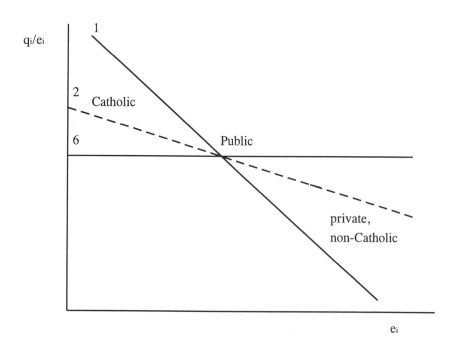

Figure 5.1
Sector Concentration Surrounding the Diminishing Returns to Expenditures (e_i) Line

But in regression six e_i is omitted and the sector parameter signs are reversed. In the transition from regression one to regression six, the reference line changes from line one to line six in figure 5.1 since the parameter for the independent variable e_i is implicitly set equal to zero. With this new reference line, the Catholic schools are now concentrated above line six and the private, non-Catholic schools are concentrated below line six. Hence, this explains the reversal of the sector parameter signs from regression one to regression six.

So what is the significance of this sign reversal? Diminishing returns to funding seems to be steeper within the public sector compared to the private sector. If the private schools were "allowed" to operate on a separate 'diminishing-returns-to-e_i' line they would be on regression line two in figure 5.1. In other words, q_i/e_i does not decrease as rapidly within the private sector as would be predicted from the theory of market competition. So if a sector-e_i interaction term was introduced in regression one, then a private advantage in maintaining a higher q_i/e_i in the context of increased funding would arise. In turn, this would likely cause the independent or isolated sector dummy variables to become statistically insignificant. In conclusion, the signs of the sector parameters in regressions one and six are determined largely by their relative positioning around the diminishing returns to funding line.

Turning now to the central question, were hypotheses one and two supported? To answer this, regression number one is used even though the qualitative conclusions do not depend on this. The question of *selection efficiency* is addressed first. Equations 5.2 and 5.3 summarize the results on *selection efficiency* using the estimated parameters for independent variables σ and σ^2.

$$(5.2) \quad \frac{q_i}{e_i} = Z - 19.6280(\sigma) + 0.5246(\sigma^2)$$

where:

Z = all remaining independent variables that are assumed theoretically and statistically constant.

$$(5.3) \quad \frac{\partial\left\{\frac{q_i}{e_i}\right\}}{\partial\sigma} = -19.6280 + 1.0492(\sigma)$$

Equation 5.2, which describes the non-linear relationship between efficiency(q_i/e_i) and selection homogeneity(σ), is illustrated in figure 5.2. As seen in this graph, the school sectors are positioned where they were expected to be.

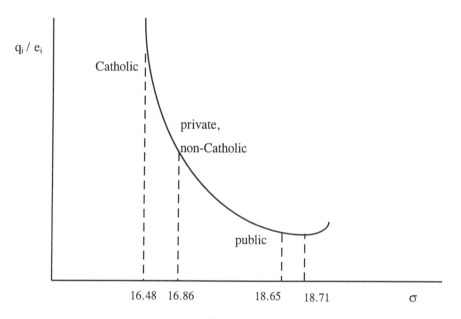

Figure 5.2
Illustration of the Estimated Negative Relationship between q_i/e_i and σ

The estimated vertex of the parabola is 18.71. Since the weighted mean for σ within each sector is less than 18.71, the general conclusion that a higher σ results in a lower q_i/e_i for all schools is justified. Therefore, hypothesis number one, concerning *selection efficiency* is supported. The estimated partial derivative for the typical school within each sector is calculated by substituting the sector mean value for σ into equation 5.3. These respective partial derivatives are listed in table 5.5.

Table 5.5
Estimated, Partial Relationship between q_i/e_i and σ
for the Typical School within Each Sector

sector	σ (mean)	$\dfrac{\partial\left\{\frac{q_i}{e_i}\right\}}{\partial\sigma}$ at mean	σ (median)	$\dfrac{\partial\left\{\frac{q_i}{e_i}\right\}}{\partial\sigma}$ at median
public	18.6547	-0.055	18.7904	0.087
Catholic	16.4820	-2.335	16.7330	-2.072
private, non-Catholic	16.8560	-1.943	12.5060	-6.507

From these results, there are four important conclusions regarding *selection efficiency*. First, the expected value for q_i/e_i for all students in a school is greater the lower the standard deviation for the ith student's school peers at the beginning of an instructional period. Second, as σ decreases, q_i/e_i increases at an increasing rate. Hence, there are increasing returns to selection homogeneity. Third, the sectors are ordered as follows with respect to the attainment of *selection efficiency*: 1)Catholic 2)private, non-Catholic 3)public. It is shown in the next chapter that the private sector values for σ are significantly lower, statistically, than the public sector values. And finally, the typical public school, for all practical purposes, is maximizing *selection inefficiency* since the mean and median value for σ is almost indistinguishable from the vertex of the parabola. Again, this is not surprising since the public school philosophy involves a "non-discriminating" and thus relatively random enrollment policy with respect to aptitude.

Next, the result for hypothesis two concerning *dynamic efficiency* is important. The independent variable $\Delta\sigma$ is intrinsically important because it measures the extent to which a school provides for distributive justice in the supply of learning capital(K_i) or cognitive growth(q_i). Instrumentally, it allows for the testing of whether more equality causes higher efficiency; and thus, whether the orthodox economic theory of learning is contradicted. Equations 5.4 and 5.5 summarize the results concerning *dynamic efficiency* using the estimated parameters for independent variables $\Delta\sigma$ and $\pm[(\Delta\sigma)^2]$ in regression number one.

(5.4) $\dfrac{q_i}{e_i}$ = W - 5.7234($\Delta\sigma$) + 1.3679$\{\pm\ [(\Delta\sigma)^2]\}$

where:

W = all remaining independent variables that are assumed theoretically and statistically constant.

(5.5) $\dfrac{\partial\left\{\dfrac{q_i}{e_i}\right\}}{\partial(\Delta\sigma)}$ = -5.7234 + 2.7358($\Delta\sigma$)

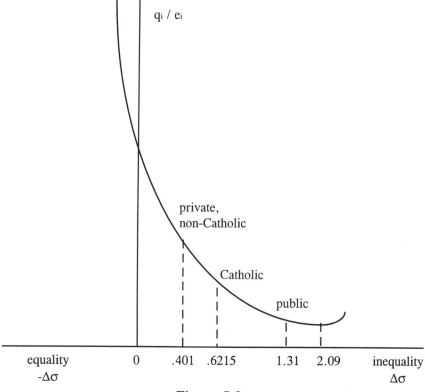

Figure 5.3
Illustration of the Estimated Negative
Relationship between q_i/e_i and $\Delta\sigma$

Equation 5.4, which describes the non-linear relationship between q_i/e_i and $\Delta\sigma$, is illustrated in figure 5.3. The positions of each school sector is again labeled. The estimated vertex of the parabola is 2.09. Since the weighted mean value for $\Delta\sigma$ within each sector is concentrated within the negatively-sloped portion of the curve, hypothesis number two, concerning *dynamic efficiency* is supported. Again, the estimated partial derivative for the typical school within each sector is calculated by substituting the sector mean value for $\Delta\sigma$ into equation 5.5. These respective partial derivatives are listed in table 5.6.

Table 5.6
Estimated, Partial Relationship between q_i/e_i and $\Delta\sigma$ for the Typical School within Each Sector

sector	$\Delta\sigma$ (mean)	$\dfrac{\partial\left\{\frac{q_i}{e_i}\right\}}{\partial(\Delta\sigma)}$ at mean	$\Delta\sigma$ (median)	$\dfrac{\partial\left\{\frac{q_i}{e_i}\right\}}{\partial(\Delta\sigma)}$ at median
public	1.31	-2.140	1.31	-2.140
Catholic	0.6215	-4.023	0.9675	-3.077
private, non-Catholic	0.401	.-4.626	-0.5435	-7.210

Several conclusions are warranted from this result. First, given element two of the orthodox economic theory of learning, the partial derivatives in table 5.6 should all be positive. In other words, there should exist a positively sloped line in figure 5.3 since a tradeoff is expected between efficiency and equality. The statistically significant result here suggests the opposite. Not only does more equality cause a higher expected q_i/e_i for *all* students within a school, it does so at an increasing rate. Again, theoretically speaking, even higher-aptitude students benefit from more equality or having their peers "catch up." Why? Because they have an increasing number of colleagues to share the costs of a high instructional target(V^*). This is the "trickle-up" effect described in chapter one. Hence, element two of the static, orthodox economic theory of learning is conceptually and empirically contradicted.

Second, to the extent that higher-aptitude pupil/families are able to "have their way" with school authorities, they can increase the mean θ_i for their entire track and increase V^* within their track. This behavior results in a higher $\Delta\sigma$ for the entire school. From this, their presumably short run gain leads to a long run loss in a lower expected q_i/e_i. Third, the sectors are ordered as follows with regard to the attainment of *dynamic efficiency*: 1)private, non-Catholic 2)Catholic 3)public. Again, it is shown in chapter six that the private sector values for $\Delta\sigma$ are significantly lower, statistically, than the public sector values. Finally, because of this ordering they are ordered the same for the production of equality over time since that is how they become *dynamically efficient*. So from this result on *dynamic efficiency*, element three of the orthodox economic theory of learning is also contradicted. Private schools weight lower-aptitude students relatively higher than public schools. There is a state failure, not a market failure in providing for equality of opportunity.

Confidence should be high with respect to the idea that smaller values for both σ and $\Delta\sigma$ *cause* a higher mean q_i/e_i within a school, ceteris paribus. The reverse-causality argument that a high q_i/e_i results in a lower σ is not persuasive since σ is a measured characteristic of a school that precedes the corresponding observed q_i/e_i in historical time. An event occurring in the future cannot cause a present event. Also, the private, non-Catholic schools had the largest values for e_i which resulted in the lowest values for q_i/e_i. At the same time, they had the lowest values for $\Delta\sigma$. Nevertheless, even with the simultaneous low efficiency rating and high equality, which is contradictory to the theory, the strong negative relationship between $\Delta\sigma$ and q_i/e_i persisted in the regression. Since the regression model reversed the conclusions that might be reached observing only raw means, the controls used in the regression model were adequate to isolate the unique opportunity costs of high aptitude dispersion and inequality.

So with respect to the first two common school goals of efficiency and equality of opportunity, private schools are superior to public schools. Within the private sector, the private, non-Catholic schools are superior to Catholic schools since they score higher in equality and *dynamic efficiency* while Catholic schools are superior in *selection efficiency* only. This overall conclusion is alarming since the most inefficient and unequal sector is also the sector having 91% of the U.S. high school enrollment in the fall of 1993.[10]

5.7   *Statistical Versus Policy Significance*

It has not been established that a policy change would lead to any significant improvement of public schools. Statistically significant parameter estimates do not imply policy significance. So to avoid making this merely an academic enterprise in evaluating competing theories, table 5.7 provides an estimate for how much the typical public school could raise its mean value for q_i/e_i by matching the private schools' lower mean values for σ and $\Delta\sigma$. These gains in mean q_i/e_i over the final two years of high school can be received in one of the following ways: i)higher achievement growth with constant expenditures, ii)constant achievement growth with lower expenditures, iii)higher achievement growth *and* lower expenditures. To calculate these percentages, a midpoint, linear approximation of the curves is used.

So if public schools imitated private schools' behavior, public schools could enjoy 17.28% more learning and 60.97% more equality over the final two years of high school with constant expenditures per-pupil(e_i). Alternatively, public schools, by imitating private schools' behavior, could maintain constant mean achievement growth(q_i) while simultaneously cutting their annual per-pupil budget(e_i) by \$972 while enjoying 60.97% more equality.

Should these potential gains for the public sector be interpreted as large and worthwhile? First, keep in mind that these gains are lower-bound estimates, especially since public-school expenditures have been under-estimated. But even this minimum estimate of the potential, public-school efficiency gain should be considered large. Pursuing a policy of lower σ and $\Delta\sigma$ is a relatively painless action that could raise intellectual growth by almost one-fifth if they merely matched the private sector and did not proceed further. It requires no summer school or increase in the average time-on-task(T_i) for students during the regular academic year. It requires no increase in capital facilities. More talented labor need not be taken from other important industries. Union-management confrontation is avoided since teacher salary and work schedules can remain constant. It does not depend on a yet-to-be-discovered pedagogical invention. Invidious comparison on a national standardized test is not used. The public school bureaucracy, at the county, state, and national levels, need not be dislodged. We can have 17.28% more achievement growth and 60.97% more equality without spending more money. Is this not a "free lunch"?

Learning Capital

Table 5.7

Estimated Efficiency and Equality Gains for the Typical Public
School if it had Private Sector Mean Values for σ and $\Delta\sigma$

Sector	Catholic	private, non-Catholic	average private
% gain in mean q_i/e_i if typical public school had mean value for σ in the respective sector.	9.42 %	6.52 %	7.91 %
% gain in mean q_i/e_i if typical public school had mean value for $\Delta\sigma$ in the respective sector.	7.70 %	11.16 %	9.37 %
Total % gain in mean q_i/e_i if typical public school had mean value for both σ and $\Delta\sigma$ in the respective sector.	17.12 %	17.68 %	17.28 %
amount of e_i that could be cut from annual public budget without lowering q_i if typical public school had mean value for both σ and $\Delta\sigma$ in the respective sector.*	$963	$994	$972
% equality gain in typical public school if they had mean value for $\Delta\sigma$ in the respective sector.	52.56 %	69.39 %	60.97 %

*calculated using 1994-1995, non-capital, expenditures per-pupil for public elementary and secondary schools($5,623). The values in this row are underestimated since it includes elementary expenditures per-pupil and excludes state and Federal administrative expenditures(*Digest of Education Statistics*, National Center For Education Statistics: U.S. Department of Education; 1995; Table 163, p. 163).

5.8 Costs of Lowering σ

What might the costs be in lowering σ in public schools at the beginning of every instructional period? Transportation costs might increase if students are traded across school district borders in order to minimize σ in all schools. An analysis of the marginal costs and marginal benefits for individual cases is necessary. Just because your favorite restaurant is ten miles across town does not mean you patronize the one nearby. Specifically, two geographically-adjacent schools each with unique instructional targets(V^*'s) and fixed budgets(e_i's), can engage in mutually-beneficial student-exchanges that increase the learning rate(K_i) for each and every participating pupil/child. Both the exiting and entering of pupils lowers σ within each school which increases the mean K_i and thus mean q_i within each school. There seem to be unexploited "gains-from-student-trade" within the public sector even with transportation costs since the private sector currently does it more aggressively. In regions with mass transit systems and beltways, the transportation costs necessary to accomplish these pareto-optimal exchanges may be negligible.

Another potential cost of minimizing σ in public schools may be hard to measure but nevertheless real. Cultural communities formed by school district borders may disintegrate and hurt both the adults' and childrens' sense of security and belonging. The sentiments attached to tradition cannot be dismissed. But contrary to this, sociologist James Coleman(1987) argues that the parish community, formed around the Catholic school and church, forms stronger and more effective social bonds. Perhaps this cost may be merely transitory since a substitute, secular community might be formed. More thought is necessary on this matter, but not here.

Some common school philosophers will balk at the idea of minimizing σ within each school in order to raise q_i/e_i. Some argue that it is good for a student to be in a school with both lower and higher achieving students. In other words, a high σ in a school is part of the socialization process. There are two responses to this position. First, there is no evidence that private school children, who study in schools with lower σ values, exhibit more anti-social behavior. And second, this argument makes the common school philosophy absurd. It is contradictory to assert that a high σ is good and at the same time be trying to minimize it over time for the sake of equality.   The result of a contradictory vision is impotence in accomplishing any of the common school goals.

It should be understood that dividing students by aptitude is not something policy makers do *to* them.   Rather, it is something done *for* them if intellectual growth is the objective.   To do otherwise is to increase marginally the average level of boredom, idleness, confusion, and anxiety, in a school with a fixed budget.   In fact, the following school illnesses may be part symptoms of a school having a large σ and thus high instructional error and low learning rates: i)truancy; ii)excessive commitment to sports, part-time jobs, and clothing fashions; iii)intellectual cynicism; iv)violence and unruliness; and v)drugs.   This assertion is supported by regressions one and two. When aptitude dispersion measures are added to regression two, the positive effect of security guards, psychologists, and counselors as a group falls 19.2%.   So a more persuasive hypothesis, concerning socialization, might be that attending a school with a large σ leads to more, not less, anti-social behavior.   To conclude, minimizing σ at the beginning of each instructional period within each school involves minor costs and major benefits.

5.9   Costs of Lowering $\Delta\sigma$

So after the optimal enrollment policy is achieved, how is the public sector to duplicate the minimum values for $\Delta\sigma$ found in the private sector and thus achieve more equality and *dynamic efficiency*? Does it even involve any cost? The public school administrator merely adopts a herding mentality. That is, the pupils are kept homogeneous in their intellectual aptitudes by employing a preferential option for the low-achieving students.

Quality teachers and instructional targets should be allocated in favor of the low-achievers.   The result of the preceding empirical analysis demonstrates that trying to instantaneously satisfy everyone equally, or having a neutral policy with respect to the allocation of θ_i and V^*, satisfies nobody over time.   More specifically, with equal allocation of resources, neither equality nor efficiency goals are enhanced over time.   Even worse, with resources disproportionately allocated to higher-aptitude pupils, the costly tutorial model becomes increasingly necessary to accommodate the increasingly-dispersed aptitudes. From this, it can be concluded that a "low-achiever bias" in resource allocation is the only reasonable option if efficiency and equality are the goals.

This "low-achiever bias" may seem frightening if it implies that higher-aptitude pupils are to remain idle while their peers are remediated. However, insofar as *selection efficiency* is maximized by minimizing σ at the beginning of an instructional period, the dereliction of these higher-achieving students with this "lower-achiever bias" approaches zero during the instructional period. Nevertheless, even with a minimum σ achieved during the enrollment stage, the "lower-achiever bias" remains necessary to prevent the growth of inequality over time.

Most important, adopting a "low-achiever bias" is relatively painless and involves no opportunity costs except the effort required to adjust the sophistication of lectures and texts incrementally downward. Most interesting is the idea that the market rewards this biased behavior because it ultimately results in a higher expected q_i/e_i for all students in a school over time. This perhaps explains why private schools are superior at producing equality. In fact, if salaries were more flexible, a market wage-premium might develop for those teachers most talented at maximizing K^* and T_i for the lower-aptitude students within each school.

However, caution must be exercised so naivete or excessive idealism doesn't creep into this analysis. Undoubtedly, some of the low-achieving students in the lowest aptitude track within a school will not respond positively to the preferential option provided them. The school administrator is confronted with the dilemma of whether to stall the growth rate of V^* on all students in order to accommodate the interests of the intractable student(s) unwilling to persevere at the track's average time-on-task(T_i). Again, creating a separate tutorial or remedial track for this student(s) is not an efficient solution.

Eventually, it becomes necessary to disregard the interests of this student by allowing V^* to proceed past the intractable student's V_i which results in a decreasing K_i for this student over time. At this point, the interests of equality and *dynamic efficiency* must yield to the interests of *selection efficiency*. The student transfers or is transferred to another school with a more optimal V^*. An analogous process would occur for the ambitious student(s) desiring V^* to accelerate past the aptitude target of the school's highest aptitude track. All schools would have both types of students. Again, the ensuing student trades would benefit all parties: the traded students, the teachers in both schools, and the peers in both schools. Trading students may appear callous. But the option currently available for students suffering high instructional error within a public school is to mentally or physically dropout or mentally or physically graduate early.

So the process of minimizing both σ and $\Delta\sigma$ in a school involves little cost and results in a more fluid and rational school system that promotes equality and higher mean cognitive growth per-hour of study, per-dollar spent. Also, teachers should find this an appealing policy. A typical complaint among teachers is that it is impossible to satisfy all their students' unique instructional needs due to the variety in their current aptitudes. Another complaint is that some pupils are behavioral or disciplinary problems and disrupt their class. This second problem may be *part* symptom of the first problem.

Before concluding this section, it is insightful to examine the potential public school gains if they matched the private sector *median* values for σ and $\Delta\sigma$. These values, which are listed in table 5.8, expand the range of possible public-school gains using the policy instruments of σ and $\Delta\sigma$.

These potential, public-school gains should be interpreted with caution since the median values are not weighted and therefore are not representative of the respective sectors. This is especially true of the private, non-Catholic sector, where a large proportion of "elite"(high admission standards) high schools were over-sampled. Also, Catholic schools with large proportions($>30\%$) of Blacks and Cuban-Hispanics were over-sampled. No doubt, the median values fall within these over-sampled strata.

Nevertheless, there seems to be no obvious reason why any high school cannot duplicate "elite" schools in their minimum values for σ and $\Delta\sigma$. Unless, perhaps, this private school advantage in *selection* and *dynamic efficiency* is achieved through the forfeiture of the third common school goal.

Table 5.8

Estimated Efficiency and Equality Gains for the Typical Public School if They had Private Sector Median Values for σ and $\Delta\sigma$

Sector	Catholic	private, non-Catholic	average private
% gain in mean q_i/e_i if typical public school had median value for σ in the respective sector.	7.41 %	73.19 %	31.80 %
% gain in mean q_i/e_i if typical public school had median value for $\Delta\sigma$ in the respective sector.	3.24 %	31.44 %	14.51 %
Total % gain in mean q_i/e_i if typical public school had median value for both σ and $\Delta\sigma$ in the respective sector.	10.65 %	104.63 %	46.31 %
amount of e_i that could be cut from annual public budget without lowering q_i if typical public school had median value for both σ and $\Delta\sigma$ in the respective sector.*	$599	$5,883	$2,604
% equality gain in typical public school if they had median value for $\Delta\sigma$ in the respective sector.	26.15 %	141.49 %	83.82 %

*calculated using 1994-1995, non-capital, expenditures per-pupil for public elementary and secondary schools($5,623). The values in this row are underestimated since it includes elementary expenditures per-pupil and excludes state and Federal administrative expenditures(*Digest of Education Statistics*, National Center For Education Statistics: U.S. Department of Education; 1995; Table 163, p. 163).

Notes

1   The data utilized in this work were made available by the Inter-university Consortium for Political and Social Research. The data for *High School and Beyond*, 1980: *Sophomore and Senior Cohort First Follow-up*(1982) were originally collected and prepared by the National Center for Educational Statistics. Neither the collector of the original data nor the Consortium bears any responsibility for the analyses or interpretations presented here.

2   The weights are calculated and applied at the individual student level using the *High School and Beyond* weighting variable, pnltstwt. It is calculated for only those students having all test results in both the base and follow-up year. The weights are calculated by taking into account the probability of the school and student being selected and actually participating. See Martin R. Frankel, Luane Kohnke, David Buonanno, and Roger Tourangeau *Sample Design Report*, National Opinion Research Center(1981) for a more detailed discussion of the weights. All regression parameters and average statistics reported are derived using weighted computations unless otherwise indicated.

3   This pupil-family-community interaction characterizes Coleman(1987) and Coleman and Hoffer's(1987) notion of "social capital" as an input to the schooling process.

4   Note that σ overestimates selection homogeneity while $\Delta\sigma$ underestimates dynamic homogeneity. This is because σ accounts for both selection homogeneity at the beginning of the students' formal education as well as equality or inequality produced by the school over the years prior to the junior year of high school or the beginning of the *High School and Beyond* Longitudinal Study. In order to assume the minimum, all of σ is assumed to be explained by selection. Finally, each school can be held fully responsible for $\Delta\sigma$ over the final two years of high school since early graduates, dropouts, and transfers are omitted from the analysis.

5   Chubb and Moe(1990) believed they were measuring the marginal impact of funding on q_i by including e_i as an independent variable. They found this parameter to be statistically no different from zero which they interpreted as a universal and unfortunate finding. However, this interpretation is problematic. The private schools, most of which were Catholic, spent relatively less while producing higher growth. The public schools, on the other hand, spent relatively more while producing relatively lower growth. Hence, the public sector observations pulled the parameter estimate toward zero.

If the sectors were analyzed separately, the marginal product of funding may be positive within the private sector. In fact, the theory of market competition leads us to expect that private schools either transformed additional funding into higher growth or the school would fail or at least not enjoy additional funding. Public schools are not subject to this force. Therefore, public schools are expected and in fact are associated with higher spending and lower output. So Chubb and Moe's(1990) production function model failed to distinguish between the public and private sector in transforming funding into growth. This oversight can be cured by using q_i/e_i as the dependent variable while controlling for diminishing returns to funding as specified in regression equation 5.1.

6   In the actual analyses, this dependent variable is multiplied by 10,000 in order to eliminate the extremely small fractions involved. If one is uncomfortable with this effective-cost ratio as the dependent variable, qi is recovered by multiplying the ratio by ei/10,000.

7   The following variables were estimated when missing: parents' socio-economic status(f_1), average hours of homework per-week(s_6), total high school enrollment(c_{10}), pupil-teacher ratio, starting teacher salary for a school, proportion of teachers with Masters or Ph.D., proportion of teachers at school over ten years, number of ability-tracks used in a school for English. The final five variables are used in regressions to be discussed.

8   Obtaining data on public school administrative expenditures per-pupil above the district level has become difficult in recent years. Up until 1980 the National Center for Education Statistics within the Department of Education published total public school expenditures per-pupil for each year in their *Digest of Education Statistics*. In 1980, they decided to interrupt this time-series and omit the state portion of administrative expenditures per-pupil. These expenditures were not placed in a separate table within their inch-thick publication that has every kind of imaginable statistic. When contacting the Department and asking why they purged this information, the following response was given: Those who re-defined this statistic are no longer employed here and are therefore unavailable for comment(paraphrased). Several questions remain: 1)Why are administrative expenditures not relevant for a full accounting of public education costs? 2)In a footnote for the relevant expenditure table it is explained that an "estimation procedure" was used to approximate the omitted expenditures in order to avoid breaking the consistency of the time-series statistic. Why must the Department estimate a number they know with certainty? 3)Was this decision made by the exiting or entering Presidential Administration?

9   There may be some concern for the low adjusted R_2 value. This level is rather typical for educational studies. For example, the largest R_2 obtained by Chubb and Moe(1990) was .053 when using only q_i as the dependent variable. It is believed .0714 is rather good since the introduction of e_i introduces extra volatility in the dependent variable. Coleman, Hoffer, and Kilgore(1985); Willms(1985); and Alexander and Pallas(1985) have R_2's around .20. However, these are obtained primarily by regressing senior test scores on sophomore test scores rather than using growth(q_i) as the dependent variable and using the sophomore score as an additional control. The regression model(5.1) used here can generate similar R_2's if senior scores are used in the numerator of the dependent variable rather than growth(q_i). However, Chubb and Moe(1990) are correct in that using only senior scores merely inflates the R_2 artificially without adding any new theoretical insight or taking full advantage of the longitudinal data in order to control for the selection bias.

10 *Digest of Education Statistics*(1995) table 55, page 68

Chapter VI

The Efficiency-Diversity Tradeoff

In the preceding chapter the theory of learning capital was empirically tested and public and private schools were compared in their attainment of common school goals one and two. Private schools were found to be more equal and more efficient. The third common school goal of integration or diversity was ignored when evaluating the sectors. A detailed analysis of integration is necessary in this chapter because efficiency and equality are not everything. Social stability could devolve if racial and socio-economic segregation was used in order to minimize σ and $\Delta\sigma$ for efficiency gains. Anarchy would make efficiency a moot issue. Therefore, educational policy should be evaluated in the context of how it either encourages or discourages the simultaneous attainment of all three common school goals.

Given this, the most clever common school policy would proceed as follows. First, a school administrator or the state would adopt a goal for the level of integration desired in each school. It could very well be the maximum that is mathematically possible given the representation of each social-group category in the general population. Once this level is understood, the school administrator *could still* proceed to minimize σ and $\Delta\sigma$ in the manner described in chapter five under the constraint to maintain the integration prescribed. For example, a predominately white school, seeking to enroll minorities, should recruit the minorities that best match the aptitudes of the school's present students. Integration should not be used as an excuse to ignore efficiency and equality. This policy would result in a school being integrated, equal, and efficient; and thus, intellectually stimulating for all pupils. This is the ideal common school. The question now is: Which schools do this best and how do they do it?

To address this question, σ and $\Delta\sigma$ become the dependent variables in regression analyses. The most important independent variables to be included in the regressions are those measuring the extent of social integration within a school. The question is whether more integration results in higher values for σ and $\Delta\sigma$ and thus a lower mean q_i/e_i within each school as hypothesized in chapter four. A corresponding empirical question is: How do the sectors compare in minimizing σ and $\Delta\sigma$ while controlling for the unique effect of integration. In order to provide answers to these two questions, the relevant mean and median values for both the dependent and independent variables to be used in the regressions are listed in table 6.1. The median value for each variable is in parenthesis. The 'non-integration' variables appearing in table 6.1 are additional explanatory variables to be used in the forthcoming regressions for σ and $\Delta\sigma$.

No conclusion can be made about relative sector performance in achieving integration or common school goal three simply by examining the mean values in table 6.1. For a sector could be completely segregated with respect to Black enrollment for example, while the mean might falsely demonstrate integration. For example, public-school X might have 100% Black enrollment while public-school Y might have 0% Black enrollment. The mean level for Black enrollment between schools X and Y would be 50% and might lead to the false conclusion that each school was 50% Black. Therefore, the mean is unreliable to assess integration performance within a sector.

The median values are unweighted, but perhaps more informative with respect to integration. Surprisingly, the median Catholic school is most integrated with respect to all of the integration categories which are: dispersion of parents' socio-economic status, % Hispanic, % Black, and % handicapped. Also, note that the median school within both private sectors have more handicapped pupils compared to the median public school. However, to the public schools' credit, the weighted, mean public school is superior to the weighted, mean, private school for all the integration categories except for handicap status.

Table 6.1
School-Level Mean and Median Integration Variables by Sector

variable		public	Catholic	private, non-Catholic
σ	mean	18.6547	16.482	16.856
	(median)	(18.7904)	(16.733)	(12.506)
Δσ	mean	1.31	0.6215	0.401
	(median)	(1.31)	(0.9675)	(-0.5435)
average sophomore composite test score in ith pupil's school		68.00 (68.36)	76.57 (75.27)	79.15 (94.81)
average socio-economic status in ith pupil's school		-26.68 (-53.88)	333.08 (276.67)	553.88 (1078.61)
socio-economic diversity: σ of the students' socio-economic status within ith pupil's school.		604.05 (601.17)	577.28 (606.45)	530.65 (481.47)
% Hispanic in ith pupil's school		.1170 (.0909)	.0885 (.1000)	.0415 (.0323)
% Black in ith pupil's school		.1020 (0.000)	.0342 (.0294)	.0187 (0.000)
% handicapped in ith pupil's school		.2373 (.2308)	.2400 (.2424)	.2871 (.2381)
pupil teacher ratio in ith pupil's school (high school enrollment(N) / number classroom teachers)		23.36 (19.07)	19.92 (19.77)	11.59 (8.10)
% of equivalent full-time staff classified as remedial specialist in ith pupil's school		.0271 (.0208)	.0177 (.0000)	.0097 (.0000)
tracking policy: number of homogeneous ability groups used for senior year English in ith pupil's school		1.939 (2)	2.144 (3)	1.165 (1)

But again, these mean values are unreliable measures for school integration just as the median values are unweighted and therefore not representative of the sector. As a result, no grand conclusion can be made concerning which sector achieves more integration. The only conclusion that might be drawn from these data is that the relative integration performance across sectors is ambiguous. Nevertheless, the *effect* integration has on σ and $\Delta\sigma$ within the typical school can be controlled using regression analysis. So the more specific empirical question to be addressed now is: Which sector maintains minimum values for σ and $\Delta\sigma$ while controlling for the impact of integration.

6.1 The Determinants of σ

Both efficiency(q_i/e_i) and equality goals require minimum values for σ and $\Delta\sigma$. As before, σ and $\Delta\sigma$ are analyzed separately. For the regression results presented in table 6.2, σ is the dependent variable. The regression observations are at the individual student level even though all the variables are school-level variables. This is done so that student weights can be applied. As a result, students enrolled in the same school have identical values for all the regression variables. The purpose of the regressions is to isolate the factors influencing a school's ability to achieve a minimum σ or *selection efficiency*, especially the level of racial, ethnic, socio-economic, and handicap integration.

There are several results to notice concerning these regressions for σ. First, without any control variables the private sector values for σ are significantly lower than the public sector values as demonstrated in regression seven. In regression eight, the mean sophomore test score within each school was used as a control for a possible ceiling-effect. In other words, σ might be low merely because all the students have become bunched at the maximum possible score. The empirical result indicates this was not the case. So after controlling for a school's mean sophomore test score, mean socio-economic status, and urban/rural location; the average private-school advantage in achieving *selection efficiency* or minimizing σ increased 33%.

Table 6.2
Regression Results for Dependent Variable σ

variable	7	8	9	10	11	12	13
intercept	18.655*** (668.90)	15.922*** (59.02)	8.031*** (15.01)	8.471*** (15.50)	10.026*** (17.92)	9.437*** (16.99)	8.468*** (15.06)
Catholic school	-2.172*** (-21.43)	-2.707*** (-26.03)	-2.575*** (-25.20)	-2.533*** (-24.77)	-2.439*** (-24.58)	-2.5733*** (-26.20)	-2.330*** (23.08)
private, non-Catholic	-1.799*** (-11.663)	-2.585*** (-16.21)	-1.976*** (-12.52)	-1.948*** (-12.34)	-1.936*** (-12.65)	-2.1875*** (-14.42)	-1.8266*** (-11.74)
mean soph. test score in ith student's school	---	0.0398*** (10.19)	0.0510*** (13.20)	0.0466*** (11.49)	0.0224*** (4.95)	0.0194*** (4.34)	0.0248*** (5.54)
mean socio-economic status for ith student's school peers	---	0.0006*** (5.45)	.0002 (1.69)	.0001 (0.90)	.0003* (2.37)	.0004*** (3.94)	.0002 (1.55)
urban school	---	-0.065 (-0.83)	-0.204* (-2.668)	-0.189* (-2.475)	0.163* (2.13)	0.2610** (3.46)	0.1364 (1.79)
rural school	---	0.1339* (2.174)	0.0771 (1.279)	0.0579 (0.960)	0.0720 (1.223)	-0.0656 (-1.122)	0.1104 (1.812)
σ of socio-econ status in ith student's school	---	---	0.0186*** (12.11)	0.0184*** (11.96)	0.0194*** (13.03)	0.0167*** (11.095)	0.0169*** (11.28)
σ^2 of socio-econ status in ith student's school	---	---	-.00001*** (-8.61)	-.00001*** (-8.38)	-.00001*** (-9.85)	-.00001*** (-8.25)	-.00001*** (-8.54)

(continued)

Table 6.2 (continued)
Regression Results for Dependent Variable σ

variable	7	8	9	10	11	12	13
% Hispanic in ith student's school	---	---	---	-0.6377	-2.2442***	-2.2965***	-2.1810***
				(-1.38)	(-4.96)	(-5.143)	(-4.90)
% Hispanic squared				-1.008	0.2505	0.3124	-0.1431
				(-1.70)	(0.434)	(0.548)	(-0.251)
% Black in ith student's school	---	---	---	---	7.9831***	8.0129***	7.9445***
					(19.81)	(20.14)	(20.02)
% Black squared		---	---		-15.529***	-15.352***	-15.222***
					(-28.86)	(-28.89)	(-28.73)
% handicap in ith student's school	---	---	---	---	---	11.945***	12.090***
						(15.421)	(15.65)
% handicap squared	---	---	---	---	---	-15.498***	-15.671***
						(-10.76)	(-10.91)
high school enrollment (N)	---	---	---	---	---	---	0.0004***
							(9.89)
adjusted R^2	0.035	0.0611	0.1005	0.1029	0.1564	0.1789	0.1839
n=student observations	15,727	15,727	15,727	15,727	15,727	15,727	15,727
F-statistic	285.99	171.51	220.73	181.33	234.72	245.68	237.24

*p-value ≤ .05   **p-value ≤ .001   ***p-value ≤ .0001   all p-values for two-tailed test

The important question is whether the private schools maintain minimum values for σ when the level of integration or diversity is controlled. Again, the variables measuring integration within each school are: i)standard deviation of a school's socio-economic status ii)% Hispanic iii)% Black iv)% handicapped. The square of each of these variables is also included. These integration variables are expected and in fact do exert a non-linear effect on σ.

As integration variables are added between regressions eight and twelve, the private advantage in minimizing σ decreases 10%. Hence, the private sector achieves some of its *selection efficiency* advantage by practicing more segregation compared to the public sector. However, it is a trivial amount. When adding high school enrollment(N) in regression thirteen, the private advantage decreases 13%. So having a smaller school explains more of the private advantage in minimizing σ than all of the integration categories combined. The main point is that the private sectors' superior performance in achieving *selection efficiency* is not primarily due to the forfeiture of integration or the forfeiture of social diversity.

Again, it is emphasized that these results suggest nothing about the actual integration levels achieved between sectors. Nor does it mean that the hypothesized tradeoff between efficiency and integration is insignificant. The average and median statistics combined with the statistically-significant, regression results suggest that a large efficiency-diversity tradeoff exists, but the sectors are approximately equal in their present integration levels.

A more useful, policy-oriented interpretation of these results for σ is offered. A school or the state could adopt any integration goal. The standards could be the current public sector integration levels or the maximum possible. Whatever they are, they could be substituted into the linear function estimated by regression thirteen. The private advantage in achieving *selection efficiency* would persist as denoted by the statistically significant and negative sector parameters. In fact, the net effect of all the control variables is to *increase* the private advantage in minimizing σ by 4.7%. So with integration controlled, private schools remain superior to public schools in achieving *selection efficiency* or maximizing mean q_i/e_i by minimizing σ. In other words, private schools integrate without significantly forfeiting *selection efficiency*.

6.2 The Determinants of $\Delta\sigma$

A similar regression analysis is now conducted for $\Delta\sigma$. The lower this variable, the more equality and *dynamic efficiency* achieved. The effects of mean student-body characteristics and integration are analyzed in regressions fifteen through eighteen. In addition, regressions nineteen and twenty test for the possible effects five school-policy variables might have on $\Delta\sigma$ during the final two years of high school.

There are several results to notice concerning these regressions for $\Delta\sigma$. Without any control variables in regression number fourteen, the private sector values for $\Delta\sigma$ are significantly lower, statistically, than public sector values. This is an important outcome, since it is difficult to gauge relevant differences when visually inspecting this raw equality variable($\Delta\sigma$).

The private advantage in equality decreases significantly with the inclusion of student-body mean characteristics in regression fifteen. The private sector advantage decreased 47% with these mean controls. But $\Delta\sigma$ remained significantly lower than the public sector values. In addition to the mean variables, σ was used as an independent variable in order to control for students regressing to the mean. In other words, the larger the proportion of students scoring both abnormally low and high on the sophomore test, the higher the chance these students shifted toward the mean on the senior test and thus lowering $\Delta\sigma$ through the basic law of conditional probability. The empirical result indicates that this was the case. Also, the Catholic sector took the lead position in minimizing $\Delta\sigma$ in regression fifteen; a position it does not lose.

Most important, how do the sectors compare in equality and *dynamic efficiency* when integration is controlled? In other words, does the private-school advantage in producing equality "wash out" when integration is controlled? Recall that the amount of equality a school is able to produce likely depends on the amount of cultural homogeneity. In other words, more integration is expected to impair a school's ability to minimize $\Delta\sigma$ due to different cultural valuations placed on formal schooling. The private advantage decreased 21% between regressions fifteen and eighteen. Hence, segregation explains a significant amount of the private advantage in equality and *dynamic efficiency*. The addition of integration variables caused the Catholic advantage to fall 18%. Whereas the private, non-Catholic advantage

Table 6.3
Regression Results for Dependent Variable Δσ

variable	14	15	16	17	18	19	20
intercept	1.310***	6.113***	7.538***	8.750***	8.674***	8.836***	8.403***
	(71.11)	(32.84)	(22.02)	(23.81)	(23.49)	(23.83)	(22.48)
Catholic school	-0.6883***	-0.4445***	-0.3902***	-0.3897***	-0.3633***	-0.4597***	-0.3374***
	(-10.28)	(-6.70)	(-5.89)	(-5.93)	(-5.50)	(-6.60)	(-4.74)
private, non-Catholic	-0.9090***	-0.3942***	-0.3429**	-0.3133*	-0.3011*	-0.2776*	-0.0197
	(-8.925)	(-3.93)	(-3.41)	(-3.13)	(-2.99)	(-2.76)	(-0.190)
mean soph. test score in school	---	-0.0310***	-0.0273***	-0.0417***	-0.0413***	-0.0391***	-0.0367***
		(-12.67)	(-11.05)	(-14.17)	(-14.04)	(-13.11)	(-12.26)
mean socio-economic status in school	---	-0.0008***	-0.0009***	-0.0008***	-0.0008***	-0.0008***	-0.0010***
		(-11.10)	(-12.42)	(-11.67)	(-11.90)	(-11.21)	(-13.07)
urban school	---	0.2314***	0.1952***	0.3820***	0.3703***	0.3582***	0.3228***
		(4.76)	(4.02)	(7.69)	(7.44)	(7.19)	(6.42)
rural school	---	0.0651	0.0570	0.0106	0.0230	0.0141	0.1386**
		(1.69)	(1.49)	(.277)	(.598)	(.366)	(3.46)
σ	---	-0.1489***	-0.1543***	-0.1666***	-0.1642***	-0.1655***	-0.1716***
		(-29.90)	(-30.46)	(-32.12)	(-31.25)	(-31.34)	(-32.54)
σ of socio-econ status in school	---	---	-0.0066***	-0.0067***	-0.0060***	-0.0062***	-0.0065***
			(-6.77)	(-6.88)	(-6.03)	(-6.29)	(-6.58)
σ2 of socio-econ status in school	---	---	.000006***	.000007***	.000006***	.000006***	.000006***
			(8.09)	(8.32)	(7.54)	(7.78)	(7.89)
% Hispanic in school	---	---	---	1.5208***	1.5132***	1.4796***	1.4046***
				(5.16)	(5.14)	(5.95)	(4.79)
% Hispanic squared	---	---	---	-2.3185***	-2.3274***	-2.2373***	-2.3004***
				(-6.17)	(-6.20)	(-5.95)	(-6.12)

*p-value ≤ .05   **p-value ≤ .001   ***p-value ≤ .0001   all p-values for two-tailed test

(continued)

Table 6.3 (continued)
Regression Results for Dependent Variable $\Delta\sigma$

variable	14	15	16	17	18	19	20
% Black in school	---	---	---	-0.5583*	-0.5492*	-0.4597	-0.7106*
				(-2.10)	(-2.07)	(-1.71)	(-2.62)
% Black squared	---	---	---	-1.7378***	-1.7544***	-1.7358***	-1.5323***
				(-4.84)	(-4.88)	(-4.75)	(-4.18)
% handicap in school	---	---	---	---	-2.0636***	-2.0701***	-2.0299***
					(-4.01)	(-4.03)	(-3.97)
% handicap squared	---	---	---	---	3.7418***	3.8070***	3.8135***
					(3.93)	(4.00)	(4.03)
e_i	---	---	---	---	---	-.00006***	-.00005***
						(-4.37)	(-4.10)
pupil-teacher ratio (N/classroom teachers)	---	---	---	---	---	-0.0002	-0.0005*
						(-1.06)	(-2.61)
% of equiv. full-time staff classified as remedial specialist (base year)	---	---	---	---	---	---	2.8414***
							(4.74)
number of ability groups for senior English	---	---	---	---	---	---	0.0853***
							(9.27)
school enrollment (N)	---	---	---	---	---	---	0.0002***
							6.81
adjusted R^2	0.011	0.1403	0.1476	0.1619	0.1627	0.1636	0.1739
n-student observations	15,727	15,727	15,727	15,727	15,727	15,727	15,727
F-statistic	88.33	367.66	303.53	234.72	204.69	181.98	166.48

*p-value ≤ .05   **p-value ≤ .001   ***p-value ≤ .0001   all p-values for two-tailed test

fell 24%. So once again, the private sector does achieve some of its advantage in equality and *dynamic efficiency* by practicing segregation.

However, once again, both private sectors remain superior to the public sector in minimizing $\Delta\sigma$ even with mean student-body and integration controls. Therefore, regression eighteen demonstrates that private schools are superior to public schools in achieving equality and *dynamic efficiency* when mean student-body characteristics and social integration variables are included.

Next, what specific school policies inhibit or enhance the production of equality and thus *dynamic efficiency*? The estimated parameter for each school policy variable is largely determined by the public sector since they have the most observations. Regression nineteen demonstrates that marginal increases in e_i lowers $\Delta\sigma$. So incremental expenditures(e_i) seem to be allocated more toward low achievers. This is an important finding since many production function studies(Hanushek, 1986, 1989; Chubb and Moe, 1990) find no direct impact of e_i on q_i. Hence, the conclusion here is that expanding educational budgets increases equality and thus *dynamic efficiency*. Notice further that if higher expenditures(e_i) are used specifically to reduce class sizes, then equality is enhanced.

Ability tracking in senior-level English exacerbates inequality and thus lowers a school's efficiency. This is not surprising since most educational studies demonstrate that tracking by ability is a self-fulfilling prophecy. Using learning capital terminology, each aptitude-track has a unique V^*. Typically, the lower the mean aptitude of the track, the slower V^* moves throughout the instructional period. It is uncertain whether this is due to the students stalling the average time-on-task(T_i), the teachers having lower standards, or both. No matter the cause, the net effect is to increase the dispersion of aptitudes between tracks over time. So the policy of tracking promotes neither equality nor *dynamic efficiency*.

Recall that school enrollment(N) had no direct impact on efficiency as demonstrated in regression one where q_i/e_i was the dependent variable. However, school size or enrollment(N) has a negative, indirect impact on both *selection* and *dynamic efficiency* as demonstrated in regressions thirteen and twenty. For equality and *dynamic efficiency* specifically, perhaps there is an insensitivity factor regarding low-achievers when larger student bodies are assembled. The main point to recognize here is that public schools are too large if schools are to be organized for purposes of efficiency and equality.

The most surprising policy result is that a higher proportion of remedial specialists results in more inequality and thus less *dynamic efficiency*. This is the opposite effect they are suppose to have. Why might this be? There is the reverse-causality theory that a higher $\Delta\sigma$ forced the school to hire more remedial specialists. However, this is not persuasive because the proportion of remedial specialists was an observation of the school's staff in the base year, before $\Delta\sigma$ occurred. Perhaps the tutorial/remedial programs are not sufficiently intense to re-integrate lower-achieving students with their higher-achieving peers. The remedial specialists may simply become de-facto teachers in separate tracks with smaller class sizes and a lower and slower moving V*. So achieving more equality and *dynamic efficiency* within the public schools is not as simple as employing relatively more teachers that specialize in compensatory or remedial education.

Finally, regression twenty had sufficient policy variables to eliminate the statistical significance of the private, non-Catholic advantage for $\Delta\sigma$ over the public sector. Hence, when mean student-body characteristics, integration, expenditures(e_i), class size, and school policies are controlled; the private, non-Catholic schools become equal to the public schools in producing equality and *dynamic efficiency*. But the fact that it took seventeen control variables to eliminate the statistical-significance of the private, non-Catholic advantage over the public school in producing equality betrays conventional wisdom. Even more, regression twenty was unable to explain all of the Catholic advantage in producing equality or minimizing $\Delta\sigma$ which remains at 25.8%.

6.3 Where are the Superior Common Schools Found?

To sum up, an inventory is taken of what has been empirically discovered in the present and preceding chapter. To do this, regressions twelve and nineteen are used for σ and $\Delta\sigma$, respectively. These regressions include only average student body characteristics, integration variables, expenditures per-pupil(e_i), and class size. The remaining independent variables are policy-oriented and thus should be excluded from a comparison of actual sector performance. Using the parameter estimates for the sector dummy variables in these two regressions; adjusted values for σ and $\Delta\sigma$ can be estimated for the private sectors. With these new estimates for σ and $\Delta\sigma$, the effect of average student-body characteristics, integration, expenditures per-pupil(e_i), and class size on the levels for σ and $\Delta\sigma$ is "filtered out."

Using these adjusted private-sector mean values for σ and $\Delta\sigma$, the public school potential gain in mean q_i/e_i by matching the still lower private-sector, adjusted, mean values for σ and $\Delta\sigma$ is re-calculated. This total potential gain for the typical public school is listed in row five of table 6.4. This newly estimated private-advantage is a more objective comparison between sectors concerning their attainment of common school goals one and two because the tradeoff between efficiency and integration is controlled. In other words, table 6.4 describes the magnitude of the private-sector advantage in efficiency and equality given the assumption that both the public and private sectors are equally integrated.

After controlling for integration, the average private *advantage* in efficiency decreased from 17.3%(table 5.7-row 3) to 14.8%(table 6.4-row 5). More specifically, the private, non-Catholic advantage over the public sector decreased the most from 17.7% to 11.3%. Whereas the Catholic advantage fell from 17.1% to 16.8%. So 14.3% of the original private advantage in minimizing σ and $\Delta\sigma$ and realizing the corresponding efficiency and equality gains was explained by integration, mean student-body characteristics, expenditures per-pupil(e_i), and class size. The private advantage fell despite the fact that the unweighted, median private schools had integrated relatively more handicap students while the unweighted, median, Catholic school was more integrated in all social categories. Perhaps this implies that the higher mean integration levels for Blacks, Hispanics, and socio-economic status within the public sector are in fact measuring legitimate integration and not merely the average between segregated schools.

Nevertheless after controlling for the effect integration has on σ and $\Delta\sigma$, the private advantage in equality and efficiency persists. This is significant since a large number of control variables have been used for the purpose of distinguishing the average behavior of public and private schools. The private sector advantage in minimizing σ persists with twelve control variables employed in regression number twelve. In addition, the private sector advantage in minimizing $\Delta\sigma$

Learning Capital

Table 6.4
Efficiency and Equality Gains for Typical Public School if it had Private Sector Adjusted Mean Values for σ and $\Delta\sigma$

Sector	Catholic	private, non-Catholic	average private
estimated private value for σ with student body controls* (public sector mean = 18.6547)	16.0814	16.4672	16.2743
% gain in mean q_i/e_i if typical public school had mean value for σ in the respective sector	12.14 %	8.75 %	11.27 %
estimated private value for $\Delta\sigma$ with student body and financial controls** (public sector mean = 1.31)	0.8503	1.0324	0.94135
% gain in mean q_i/e_i if typical public school had estimated mean value for $\Delta\sigma$ in the respective sector	4.62 %	2.54 %	3.54 %
Total % gain in mean q_i/e_i if typical public school had estimated mean value for both σ and $\Delta\sigma$ in the respective sector	16.76 %	11.29 %	14.81 %
amount of e_i that could be cut from annual public budget without lowering q_i if typical public school had estimated mean value for both σ and $\Delta\sigma$ in respective sector***	$ 942	$ 635	$ 833
% equality gain in typical public school if it had estimated mean value for $\Delta\sigma$ in the respective sector	35.09 %	21.19 %	28.14 %

*   control variables are: mean sophomore test score, mean socio-econ status, urban/rural, σ of socio-econ status, % Black, % Hispanic, % handicapped, each integration variable squared.

**   control variables are: mean sophomore test score, mean socio-econ status, urban/rural, σ, σ of socio-econ status, % Black, % Hispanic, % handicapped, e_i, class size, each integration variable squared.

**** calculated using 1994-1995, non-capital, expenditures per-pupil for public elementary and secondary schools($5,623). The values in this row are underestimated since it includes elementary expenditures per-pupil and excludes state and Federal administrative expenditures(*Digest of Education Statistics*, National Center For Education Statistics: U.S. Department of Education; 1995; Table 163, p. 163).

persists with fifteen control variables employed in regression number nineteen. On top of these controls for σ and $\Delta\sigma$, twenty-four control variables were employed in regression number one in order to isolate the unique influence σ and $\Delta\sigma$ had on q_i/e_i.

So what is the significance of the numerous control variables in these regressions? It is difficult to eliminate both the efficiency-enhancing effects of minimum values for σ and $\Delta\sigma$ as well as the private advantage in minimizing σ and $\Delta\sigma$. This leads to the conclusion that the efficiency and equality gap between public and private schools is explained by the unique incentives encountered within the state and market sectors. The differential behavior between a public and a private school is not due to chance.

To summarize, a ranking of the school sectors are made with regard to their simultaneous attainment of all the common school goals using the results listed in table 6.4. The logic proceeds as follows. Regression nineteen demonstrates that the private sectors' mean value for $\Delta\sigma$ is significantly lower than the public sector's mean value even with integration controlled. Thus, the private sector is more equal(table 6.4-row 7) which is the second common school goal. Regressions twelve and nineteen reveal that the private sectors' mean values for both σ and $\Delta\sigma$ are significantly lower than the public sector mean value even with integration controlled. Thus, the private sector is more efficient(table 6.4-row 5) which is the first common school goal. Finally, the private-sector advantage in efficiency and equality holds no matter the social composition or integration levels in the respective sectors which is the third common school goal. This conclusion that the best common schools are found in the private sector is outlined below:

1) Maximum average cognitive achievement growth per-dollar spent per-pupil. Or similarly, maximum expected value for q_i/e_i within the school.

    row five of table 6.4:   i) Catholic
                                           ii) private, non-Catholic
                                           iii) public

2) Equality of educational opportunity; or more strongly, a minimum $\Delta\sigma$ within the school.

row seven of table 6.4:   i) Catholic
                             ii) private, non-Catholic
                             iii) public

3) Integration of students from different ethnic, racial, socio-economic, and handicap backgrounds.

normalized by integration control variables in regressions twelve and nineteen and therefore equalized between sectors.

So the original assertion that the private sector is superior in the simultaneous attainment of all the common school goals is justified. The source of the private-school advantage is no mystery. Private schools minimize instructional error using the least-cost strategy. Part of this strategy is to minimize σ while maintaining constant integration, an enrollment policy available for any school. The remaining part of the strategy is to produce more equality or use goal two as the impetus for goal one. On the margin, public schools either ignore instructional error or expand the number of expensive tracks while ignoring the more just and efficient tools of σ and $\Delta\sigma$.

These empirical results are best summarized with a story. One hundred sophomores are selected from the general student population. They are representative of the general population with respect to race, ethnicity, socio-economic status, handicap status, and current achievement levels. Over the final two years of high school each student agrees to study T_i hours per-week. Each pupil/family also pays e_i for their respective educations. The subjects to be studied are reading, writing, vocabulary, science, mathematics, and civics. Benevolent government leaders must decide whether to place them in the public or private sector. If placed in the private sector, the students will learn 14.81% more over the two years. Part of the reason each student learns more is because their achievement levels will be 28.14% more equal on graduation day.

To conclude using economic jargon, the public schools' 14.81% lower efficiency rating is deadweight loss that vanishes into the atmosphere. The public schools' higher values for σ and $\Delta\sigma$ generate excess heat and thus causes energy loss from their educational engines. This excess heat and resulting energy loss is unnecessary levels of redundancy, idleness, confusion, and anxiety caused by high aptitude dispersion and the corresponding budget dilemma caused by instructional error. Paradoxically, part of this deadweight loss in the public sector may be due to using the orthodox economic theory of learning; originally intended to maximize social efficiency through the regrettable but necessary policy of allocating relatively more resources toward higher aptitude pupils.

Chapter VII

School Excellence: A Purely Rational Pursuit of Efficiency?

Thus far the school has been described as a mere business enterprise organized by the administrator for the purpose of maximizing mean cognitive achievement growth per-pupil expenditures(q_i/e_i). This simplification permitted a fruitful exercise in deductive logic. The policy instruments of σ and $\Delta\sigma$ were found to be the cheapest means for attaining the rational ends of a school. Further, private schools were found to be the leaders in achieving *selection* and *dynamic efficiency*. The implicit conclusion has been that market forces caused private school administrators to behave more rationally. This market-induced rationality resulted in superior common schools.

This economic story is believed to be, for the most part, true. However, the rational-actor model may not explain all of the empirical results. Four plausible alternative hypotheses for explaining the sector differentials for σ and $\Delta\sigma$ are now offered. They are presented for two reasons. First, it is not believed that all education decisions are made using the cost-benefit calculus. And second, the actual effect of educational policy may partly depend on whether these alternative theories of causality explain part of the whole.

7.1 Aptitude Drift Hypothesis

Public schools had high values for $\Delta\sigma$ or inequality. Part of the explanation was that the parents of higher-aptitude students were able to petition the school to increase V^* which eventually causes a higher $\Delta\sigma$. This "high-achiever bias" was attributed to the "voice" mechanism and politics. This account may be inadequate.

Assume the typical public-school classroom had students with aptitudes represented by a, b, and c in figure 7.1. The teacher is initially employing a preferential option for the low-achievers as illustrated by V^* being in the southwest portion of the solid-line aptitude space. Every year the teacher in this classroom maintains the same curriculum or V^* with every student cohort since new students have always been adequately prepared for the instructional target V^*. Or each student cohort has consistently been characterized by aptitudes a, b, and c.

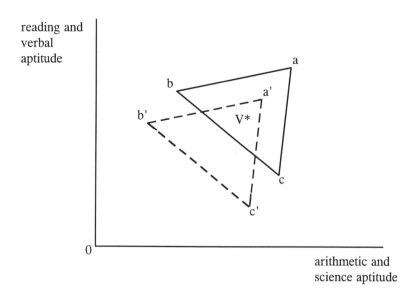

Figure 7.1
Illustration of Aptitude Drift

Now suppose students in the lower-grade cohort independently lowered the amount of homework they did. Perhaps they increased their television viewing, visited the mall more frequently, and concentrated more on sports; all at the expense of time-on-task(T_i). This is consistent with a culture whose time has become precious(Becker, 1965; Linder, 1970). With more total activities, less time is spent on each individual activity. So less time is spent on the individual activity of school. Hence, these new students begin the year with lower aptitudes than previous students in previous years. The new students' aptitudes are now illustrated by a', b', and c' in figure 7.1. The students' aptitudes drifted southwesterly due to their historically lower levels of time-on-task(T_i).[1]

It is highly probable the instructional target(V^*) remains constant. New texts were not purchased. The teacher's notes are still used. State mandated curriculums may even require V^* to remain constant. The school might be determined to maintain high "academic standards." And V^* even continues to be pareto optimal as earlier defined. However, the students' learning rates(K_i) are now positively related to the students' aptitudes(V_i); whereas in previous years there was a negative relationship.

The point is that V^* becomes biased for the higher-aptitude students without any political influence by parents. It happened because the students' aptitudes changed, not V^*. The problem now is that $\Delta\sigma$ will increase since the higher-aptitude students now enjoy relatively higher learning rates. The result is more inequality and lower *dynamic efficiency*. Thus, less cognitive growth(q_i) occurs on the average in the present year with the given school budget. When this student cohort is promoted to the next grade level, also characterized by a historically fixed V^*, inequality and inefficiency accelerates since the lower present mean achievement growth(q_i) exacerbates negative aptitude drift. So average cognitive growth stagnates further each year even if average time-on-task(T_i) remains constant in subsequent instructional periods.

The acceleration of inequality in the public schools measured by a large mean value for $\Delta\sigma$ observed in the *High School and Beyond* Data from 1980-1982 may be one particular observation in a long, secular trend caused by aptitude drift. Most important, it was not explained by the political influence of parents of high-aptitude students. So a high $\Delta\sigma$ across both public and private sectors may be explained by aptitude drift. But on the other hand, it does not explain the private *advantage* in minimizing $\Delta\sigma$. So the political-voice theory may still be valid since the private schools were under the same historical force of lower T_i's. Nevertheless, for the entire school system, it is vital that V^* be quickly adjusted downward when aptitudes fall. If a school system is inflexible and slow in responding to a small, initial downward drift in aptitudes; all subsequent learning is thrown into convulsions since inequality and thus inefficiency accelerates over time.

7.2 *Unintentional Student Sorting*

Private schools had lower values for σ and thus enjoyed more *selection efficiency*. It was explained that private school administrators deliberately sorted students or minimized s using transcript information or entrance examination results.

It is perhaps possible for no aptitude information to be gathered and still achieve a relatively lower σ in private schools. The fact that parents are willing and able to pay private school tuition means that the parents are of relatively high socio-economic status. Households with higher socio-economic status have children with relatively higher aptitudes. As a result, only high-aptitude pupils enroll in the private school. Tuition acts as a sorting mechanism that indirectly lowered σ. Hence, the private schools' *selection efficiency* advantage may not be due to deliberate, rational, policy-making.

Similar reasoning can be applied to the few public schools that had a low σ. Neighborhoods can be distinguished by home prices. The more expensive the homes, the higher the socio-economic status of parents and the higher the aptitudes of their children. So home prices and zoning regulations may also act as a sorting mechanism that lowers σ in a school district defined by geography. Families are then brought together that share similar instructional needs(Tiebout, 1959; Oates, 1969; Hamilton, 1976). Evidently, this was not a sufficiently strong force to match the lower values for σ found in the private sector. To conclude, a minimum σ may have been an accident caused by homogeneous home prices or high tuition, not consciously minimized by school administrators. Nevertheless, lessons learned through historical accident should not be forgotten.

7.3 The Possibility of Losing Your Friends

Again, private schools were more equal or had lower values for $\Delta\sigma$ compared to public schools. The rationale was that private schools allocated a disproportionate amount of resources toward initially lower achievers. This may not necessarily be the case.

Parents make a big expenditure decision when they elect to send their child to a private school. The marginal cost of the public school is zero. For the private school it is the tuition. Because of this, parents are sensitive to the differential benefits of each school. Perhaps they believe their child will enjoy a higher learning rate in the private school due to having a more optimal V^* or minimum instructional error.

Now suppose a student falls behind his private school peers and begins to have a lower rate of learning due to negative instructional error($\|V_i < V^*\|$). Parents become aware of this and conclude that the public school has a more optimal instructional target. Returning to the public school would result in a higher rate of learning(K_i) and private school tuition savings.

However, the student does not want to transfer because he has developed a network of friends in the private school. To avoid this transfer, the student either obtains private tutoring or perseveres in an intense self-tutorial in order to catch up with his private school peers. Even the mere threat of this occurring might encourage all students to avoid falling behind. The result is a lower relative $\Delta\sigma$ for private schools that was not due to the specific budget policy of the school. It should be understood that this alternative theory does not contradict the idea of *dynamic efficiency*. It merely alters the explanation for why the private sector might be superior in achieving it.

7.4 Profit-Maximization and Christian Philosophy

Finally, Catholic schools were most effective in transforming a given level of funding(e_i) into a large learning rate(K_i) and thus high cognitive growth(q_i) after controlling for integration. The implied motive was to survive financially by attracting students and the corresponding revenue. This is obviously a caricature for religious schools whose motives are more noble. However, this does not mean that efficiency is trivialized by the Catholic church:

> The church acknowledges the legitimate role of profit as an indication that a business is functioning well. When a firm makes a profit, this means that productive factors have been properly employed and corresponding human needs have been duly satisfied.... Profit is a regulator of the life of a business, but it is not the only one; other human and moral factors must also be considered which, in the long term, are at least equally important for the life of a business.
> - John Paul II, *Centesimus Annus*(1991) pp. 68-69

Coincidentally, one of these other moral factors, distributive justice or a minimum $\Delta\sigma$, causes efficiency in the production of education. Because of this, both the Catholic school administrators' and teachers' religious beliefs may be uniquely suited for the provision of equal and thus efficient education. Given this possibility, four elements of Catholic philosophy are now analyzed that are perhaps instrumental in making for superior common schools.

First, the intellectual life is a relatively important vocation for the Catholic. One implication of being made in the image of God(Genesis, 1:27) is to be granted a spiritual dimension or soul where the intellect resides. The pursuit of truth, knowledge, wisdom, justice, and beauty is essentially a spiritual enterprise devoted to growing closer to God, the creator of humankind and the natural universe. However, this academic vocation requires discipline, perseverance, and grace since the intellect has been damaged by sin:

> God has given to man the power of reason, and he expects man to use this gift. There are two ways in which the power of reason may be abused. One way is not using it.
> - Leo J. Trese, *The Faith Explained*(1965) p. 139

> man, as sharing in the light of the divine mind, rightly affirms that by his intellect he surpasses the world of mere things... For his intellect is not confined to the range of what can be observed by the senses. It can, with genuine certainty, reach to realities known only to the mind, even though, as a result of sin, its vision has been clouded and its powers weakened.
> - *Pastoral Constitution on the Church in the Modern World(Guadium et spes) #15*

Man whole and entire, soul united to body in unity of nature, with all his faculties natural and supernatural, such as right reason and Revelation show him to be; man, therefore fallen from his original estate, but redeemed by Christ and restored to the supernatural condition of adopted son of God...
- Pius XI *"The Christian Education of Youth"*(1939)

The beauty of truth, the refining and elevating influences of knowledge, are meant for all, and she[the church] wishes them to be brought within the reach of all. Knowledge enlarges our capacity both for self-improvement and for promoting the welfare of our fellow men; and in so noble a work the church wishes every hand to be busy.
- Third Baltimore Council(1884); reprinted in *Catholic Education in America: A Documentary History*(McClusky, ed., 1964)

With this educational philosophy one is less inclined to abandon a pupil using the rationale of inferior reasoning potential. It is more developmental and thus more confident and ambitious compared to the screening model(Spence, 1973; Layard and Psacharopoulos, 1974; Stiglitz,1975; Wolpin, 1977) where the belief is that pupils have different and permanent abilities and the school's function is to merely identify these pupils for industry and higher education.

Another relevant idea within Catholic philosophy does not pertain specifically to education. With regard to the Church's moral teaching on the economic order, it is asserted that a "preferential option for the poor"(National Conference of Catholic Bishops, 1986) should guide all policy. This ideal comes from scripture where Jesus' first public utterance was: "The spirit of the Lord is upon me, because he has anointed me to preach the good news to the poor(Luke 4:18)." Jesus' emphasis on those in need leads to the following Church position:

It...demands a compassionate vision that enables the Church to see things from the side of the poor and powerless and to assess lifestyles, policies, and social institutions in terms of their impact on the poor.
- National Conference of Catholic Bishops, *Economic Justice For All*(1986, p. 29)

This "preferential option for the poor" coincides nicely with the need to exercise a "bias for the low-achievers" when setting the school's instructional target(s) for purposes of justice and efficiency. Recall that Catholic schools had the lowest mean value for Δσ which made them most effective with the lowest achievers. By implication, they were most effective with Black, Hispanic, handicap, and low socio-economic students since these pupils are concentrated below the mean within each school.[2] So their success may be better explained by their Christian philosophy and not unique insight into the determinants of school efficiency. In fact, given the preceding philosophy, Catholic schools may have targeted low-achievers even if it was inefficient or costly to do so.

Third, the idea that equality of educational outcomes causes higher efficiency is a strange notion to economists trained to expect the opposite. Perhaps it is neither strange nor even coincidental to an individual applying moral criteria for decisions. It might be interpreted as a particular instance of divine providence where one is not financially hurt in the long run for doing the right thing:

Justice will bring about peace; right will produce calm and security...
- (Isaiah, 32:17)

the universe is not a gigantic mixing bowl in which entities are scrambled haphazardly but a true cosmos moving with order and headed in a meaningful direction... Its primary intention is to affirm that God provides what is needed for the realization of his plans... But providence is not a license to be negligent, as though we could count on God to care for us regardless of what we do. It is through natural agencies that God ordinarily works, and our own planning and effort are among the natural factors he uses. If we neglect what depends on us, providence itself will let us fail, to teach us a lesson.
- Rev. Edward D. O'Connor, C.S.C.; *The Catholic Vision*(1992)

It is possible for the financial accounts to be in order, and yet for the people - who make up the firm's most valuable asset - to be humiliated and their dignity offended. Besides being morally inadmissible, this will eventually have negative repercussions on the firm's economic efficiency.
- John Paul II, *Centesimus Annus*(1991) pp. 68-69

So once again, at least in education, there seems to be a natural harmony between distributive justice, efficiency, and thus profits in a reasonably competitive market. This might be interpreted as providential; for the common element promoting all three is the minimization of $\Delta\sigma$ or production of equality. Interpreted from the negative side, large amounts of inequality or injustice produced within a school has long-run, "negative repercussions" on a school's efficiency(q_i/e_i) which may lead to bankruptcy.

The final element of Catholic philosophy which perhaps influences their actual behavior concerns the Christian virtue of humility. Recall that the method for producing equality is to keep the instructional target(V^*) at the level of the lower aptitude students' during initial instructional periods. This policy may be counter to intellectual desire or intellectual pride. Some teachers are rewarded by allowing them to teach highly advanced courses. A high V^* is perhaps prestigious for a school and a teacher since there is a certain honor in being on the frontier of knowledge. No doubt, a high V^* is eventually warranted for efficiency reasons so long as it is not embraced prematurely. A premature setting of a high V^* scatters students' aptitudes, invites instructional error, and thus stagnates average cognitive growth. So without an initial humble supply of V^*'s a school deteriorates. This principle of educational technology might again be understood in the context of either natural law or Revelation: "For whoever exalts himself will be humbled, and whoever humbles himself will be exulted(Matthew 23:12, Luke 18:14)."[3]

In summary, the rigors of market competition may be insufficient in explaining the efficiency of Catholic schools. Secular, private schools may not have the intangible, "spiritual" resources to compete with religious schools in minimizing $\Delta\sigma$. Strong motivation for including everybody in the efficient pursuit of knowledge may not be for sale at the secular store for educational inputs. This missionary energy is likely available in many religions; including and not necessarily limited to the Catholic, Protestant, and Jewish Traditions. Related to this, a reply might perhaps be given to Reverend Greeley's(1982, p.106) sarcastic challenge: "Educational economists have not exactly broken down the doors of Catholic institutions in their efforts to discover where Catholic school administrators buy their mirrors." The answer might be that there exists a harmony between religious principles and the peculiarity of production technology in education.

Insofar as this theological theory of causality is true, then the following policy inference follows: A nation's school system will be more efficient and more equal the larger the ratio of religiously-affiliated schools to secular schools no matter whether the secular schools are private or public. Religiously-affiliated schools may have a comparative advantage in educational production. It is not due to a large natural-resource endowment; but rather, it is attributable to beliefs which influence behavior.

The significance of religious beliefs might be understood better by discussing the role of school revenue. For a religiously-affiliated school, perhaps revenue is viewed merely as a means to keep the staff employed in their educational mission. Alternatively, revenue might be viewed as an end in itself in a more secular, profit-seeking school. In other words, in a profit-seeking school a portion of the revenue is used to produce the minimum level of education necessary to maintain enrollment and thus the revenue stream. The remaining portion of the revenue is skimmed as shareholder profits. The crucial question is whether this minimum education produced by a profit-seeking school is still larger than what the public, non-profit schools produce. The evidence from the *High School and Beyond* Data from 1980 to 1982 reveals that both religious and non-religious, private schools produce higher and more equal achievement compared to the non-profit, public schools.

Finally, this religious theory is merely an alternative hypothesis for explaining the differential behavior of religious and non-religious schools; it is not a conclusion. The rigors of market competition may still explain even the religious schools' advantage in offering efficient and equal education. Even religious schools must compete on purely practical matters of efficient secular learning. For example, this religious theory is not as persuasive in explaining σ or *selection efficiency*.

Realistically, all four alternative hypotheses offered in this chapter may be partially valid in accounting for the sector differentials in σ and $\Delta\sigma$. But in the interest of making a firm conclusion: Market forces encourage minimum values for σ and $\Delta\sigma$ no matter the motive or ultimate explanation.

Notes

1 This negative drift in standardized test scores at all education levels since the 1960's is well documented.

2 Coleman, Hoffer, and Greeley(1985) were unsuccessful at demonstrating this "common-school" effect for the disadvantaged within Catholic schools. Using q_i as the dependent variable, they ran separate regressions for Blacks and Hispanics, low socio-economic status pupils, and low sophomore achieving pupils. They found a positive and much larger parameter for the Catholic sector dummy variable for each of the three groups relative to the overall regression. However, the parameter was statistically significant only in the regression for minorities. Dividing the sample made the estimators inefficient for all three regressions and prevented a strong conclusion concerning the common-school effect. The superior common-school effect of the Catholic sector is reached here by: 1) Using $\Delta\sigma$ as a comparison, dependent variable across sectors; and 2) Using the inference or definition that disadvantaged students are concentrated below the mean in all schools.

3 Bryk, Lee, and Holland(1993) recognize this attitude when interviewing Catholic school teachers: "Teachers often used such language as 'an opportunity to serve' to describe the teaching of remedial classes. No one described such work as a consequence of his or her low status within the organization(p. 132)."

Chapter VIII

Summary of the Determinants for Common School Excellence

The theoretical and empirical conclusions concerning educational production in the United States are now summarized. Following this chapter on the determinants of school excellence, a specific program of action is outlined in chapter nine that is expected to improve education. To start, the large literature on the educational production function leads to the conclusion that schools have little impact on a pupil's education(Coleman, et. al.; 1966 - through - Hanushek, 1986, 1989). Family influences dominate while traditional school inputs are largely superfluous. Perhaps only implicitly, these results lead to the conclusion that teachers are baby-sitters, skill-identifiers, and resource allocators.

Contrary to this, the theory of learning capital makes the school once again relevant in the production and distribution of intellectual growth(q_i). A teacher is a professional whose craft involves the maximization of a pupil's learning rate(K_i) by being academically competent and privy to students' complex and changing aptitudes. However, insofar as schools are organized in a fashion that increases σ and $\Delta\sigma$, even the best teachers will have a negligible impact on students' cognitive development. The larger the proportion of pupils above and below the aptitude of the targeted pupil, the more useless even the most competent teacher's services become due to a larger aggregate level of redundancy and confusion.

So obtaining and retaining quality teachers through high expenditures per-pupil(e_i) in a school is a necessary but not a sufficient condition for maximizing mean achievement growth. A quality teaching staff must also be provided pupils with similar aptitudes. So the context under which additional expenditures per-pupil(e_i) are made is just as important as making more expenditures. As long as σ and $\Delta\sigma$ remain high in public schools, the marginal and average impact of funding will remain quite low. With high levels for σ and $\Delta\sigma$ within a single school, either average instructional error(μ) is too high in a few aptitude tracks or the school's budget and thus teachers' time is spread thinly across too many aptitude tracks.

More specifically, the following five propositions are believed both theoretically reasonable and empirically corroborated using the theory of learning capital and the *High School and Beyond* Data:

1) A student learns more when enrolled in a school with peers of similar aptitude. Or similarly, the expected value for q_i/e_i throughout an instructional period increases the smaller the value for σ at the beginning.

2) A student learns more throughout an instructional period the more equal the student's peers become in achievement during the same time period. In other words, the expected value for q_i/e_i increases as $\Delta\sigma$ decreases. Thus, no tradeoff exists between equality of opportunity and efficiency. More strongly, equality of outcomes causes higher efficiency within a school.

3) A tradeoff exists between social diversity and efficiency. Or, as integration with respect to minorities, socio-economic status, and handicap status increases, σ and $\Delta\sigma$ also increase, which in turn lowers the expected value for q_i/e_i. So diversity is a good that must be purchased with less q_i or more e_i or both.

4) Public schools can potentially lower their values for σ and $\Delta\sigma$ and thus increase efficiency without forfeiting any integration. Private schools provide the model for this possibility.

5) Private schools are superior to public schools in the simultaneous attainment of the three common school goals. Hence, market forces are more harmonious with the attainment of the common school goals of efficiency and equality compared to the political forces within state-operated schools. This conclusion is predicated on the assumption that minimum integration levels are prescribed and enforced by the state.

These five conclusions and the corresponding policy proposal to be discussed in the next chapter ultimately depend on six presuppositions of the argument: 1) Instructional error is a legitimate concept for understanding learning. 2) The typical student has the physiological capacity to learn and develop her intellect if provided appropriate instruction. 3) Students' time and parents' income are limited or scarce. 4) There are competing ends for students' time and parents' income. 5) Schools have scarce resources due to 3 and 4. 6) School administrators and teachers should do the best they can with scarce resources. These assumptions are believed reasonable. Also, the conclusions derived from these premises have been empirically corroborated.

The preceding conclusion that public schools have not been the "great equalizer" as envisioned by Horace Mann is not a surprise to radical social scientists. In fact, this theory of learning capital reaches two of the same conclusions that Bowles and Gintis(1976) reach in their classic work *Schooling in Capitalist America*. First, they argue that public schools reproduce privilege partly through ability tracking. The more recent evidence on the determinants of inequality($\Delta\sigma$) in public schools supports this diagnosis. A larger number of ability tracks used for senior-level English results in more school inequality(regression twenty). Bowles and Gintis(1976, chapter 4) also argue that the accepted educational philosophy is characterized by too much "I-Q ism." Distinguishing students by their natural intellectual abilities or natural learning rates in order to efficiently allocate scarce resources is a mistaken exercise. The theoretical and empirical results of Mastery Learning and learning capital supports Bowles and Gintis'(1976) earlier theme. But with these two ideas the similarities between the present work and Bowles and Gintis(1976) end.

Bowles and Gintis(1976, chapter eleven) conclude that the source of unequal opportunity within primary and secondary education is the capitalist mode of production that needs the social classes somehow reproduced in order to maintain political stability. This is their "correspondence" principle derived from the materialist view of history. However, given the analysis here, Bowles and Gintis(1976) appear to be half right. Comparatively speaking, the public schools do reproduce privilege or inequality within the United States. But the capitalist mode of production is not the ultimate cause of unequal education. Rather, it is the cure. Private schools, operating under the rules of private property and market competition, produce *more* equality and *higher* mean cognitive growth(q_i) relative to state schools no matter the concentration of minorities, low-income, or handicap pupils. So it would seem that the path for attaining more distributive justice within education is not to abolish capitalism, as Bowles and Gintis(1976, chapter eleven) propose, but to embrace it more fully.

Given all this, what specific educational policies should be enacted? Should the public schools be retained but merely managed like private schools? One should be suspicious of the notion that public schools just need to define their goals more clearly and then implement the rational policies designed to achieve them. The main tenet of their vision has always been equality. For this, they get high marks for intentions, but low marks for performance. Also, there is no paucity in technical ideas for obtaining educational excellence in our schools. In 1990, 14.1% of all undergraduate and graduate degrees awarded by institutions of higher education in the United States were in education pedagogy; or in other words, the study of the educational production function.[1] Finally, the fact that increasing the number of remedial specialists in a public school exacerbates inequality(regression twenty) and thus inefficiency(regression one) means the school is suffering from poor incentives not lack of ideas. The evidence presented here demonstrates the potential for large private and social gains from a policy of competition through choice.

So why has choice not been adopted if there seem to be so many obvious benefits? One of the more articulate criticisms of market competition and corresponding defense of the public school has been given by Breneman(1983) using Hirschman's(1970) distinction between the exit and "voice" mechanism for communicating dissatisfaction to an organization.

If a principal and teachers within a particular school are already inclined to be slothful and resistant to change, it seems unlikely that the loss of a few students would suddenly force them to change their ways. Indeed, the departure of those parents who care and complain will simply make life easier for all concerned. The only hope for change in such a school - the presence of a group of concerned parents who will keep prodding and pushing for improvement - will be gone, but the school will survive, stunting the lives of those students unfortunate enough to remain. Could anyone defend this outcome as a desirable public policy, reflecting the presumed benefits of competition?

- David W. Breneman "Where Would Tuition Tax Credits Take Us?" in *Public Dollars for Private Schools*(eds. Thomas James and Henry Levin, 1983)

An unnamed author from *The Economist*(1992) Magazine, echoes Brenemen's(1983) theme:

The third problem is the difficulty of combining market mechanisms with social justice. The most obvious free-market solution to educational failure is to stop financing institutions and start financing people: ie, to introduce vouchers.... . But critics argue that vouchers will help the rich(by making it easier for them to send their children to independent schools) and undermine social cohesion(by trapping poor children in sink schools).

- Anonymous Author "A Survey of Education," *The Economist*(November, 21; 1992) p. 18

Both Breneman(1983) and the author from *The Economist* (1992) believe that the less vocal, perhaps lower-aptitude pupil/families benefit from the presence of the more articulate, mostly higher-aptitude pupil/families. If the more active, higher-aptitude pupil/families were to exit a public school, then that school would become a "sink school" that "stunts" the education of lower-aptitude, lower socio-economic pupils.

But the evidence is contrary. In the private schools where exit is a legitimate option for the most quality-sensitive families, equality and thus *dynamic efficiency* is greatest. In the public schools where voice is predominant and quality-sensitive families remain relatively captive, inequality and *dynamic inefficiency* results. Hence, voice, a captive student-body, and democratic-political-control of a school is strongly and positively associated with inequality and inefficiency.

This is not surprising if one imagines how voice is actually played out in detail within a public school. Would the vocal parents of high-aptitude pupils try to increase *c-efficiency, selection efficiency,* or *dynamic efficiency*? Breneman(1983) and *The Economist*(1992) author assume they will enhance *c-efficiency* and therefore benefit all students. This is possible but not probable. First, they would only target the *c-efficiency* within their own child's track. And second, it would be awkward and costly for them to discourage bureaucracy, encourage teachers to be more competent, and draw attention to new educational technology. Similarly, using voice to increase *selection efficiency* would involve a significant lobbying of state legislators and a major disruption of traditional public-school enrollment policies. So using voice to increase a school's overall *c-efficiency* and *selection efficiency* involves minimal individual return and major time and organizational costs and is thus unrealistic(Olson, 1965).

The path of least political resistance, minimum costs in time, and maximum short-run return for voice is the dangerous route of altering θ_i and V^*. Specifically, if a "gifted and talented" program is offered, then less funding is available for middle and lower-aptitude students. If parents can get calculus offered, perhaps basic math has to be eliminated. If the most skillful English teacher with the highest homework standards is teaching college-preparatory composition, then she is perhaps not teaching basic grammar. If a teacher has both a high and a low-aptitude course and parents of high-aptitude students are complaining; which course receives the larger portion of scarce teacher attention in preparation, grading, and prodding students? In pursuit of a quiet life within their monopoly, public-school administrators and teachers marginally adjust the curriculum upward in order to satisfy higher-aptitude pupil/families at the expense of their lower-aptitude peers.

This issue of intra-school allocation of resources(θ_i and V^*) is not a new concern. The omission of intra-school budget allocation(θ_i) was Bowles'(Harvard Educational Review, 1968) critique of the original Coleman, et. al.(1966) study:

> the measurement of school resources(district expenditures per-pupil) in the survey appears to me to be highly inadequate... . School to school differences within a district were simply ignored. Even those inputs which were measured on a school-by-school basis are subject to some of the same measurement errors because the use of these

measures necessarily ignores differences in the amount of resources devoted to children in different tracks within the same school.

As a general principle, within a school where the articulate parents' curriculum desires are met and only a limited number of courses can be offered due to scarce resources; lower and perhaps middle-aptitude pupils are implicitly encouraged into study hall and more physical education courses and out of the thought track. This is perhaps done under the guise of the natural learning-rate ideology. Simply put, not all students have the same supply interests with respect to instructional targets. A choice between an advanced and beginners writing course is simply no choice at all for the more typical pupil having a medium writing aptitude. For purposes of efficiency and justice, what is offered is just as important as what is not offered. The problem is that the lower-aptitude and lower socio-economic status pupil/families suffering from the voice mechanism undercutting their supply of high learning rates are the least able to recognize and articulate the problem. Because of this, they need the exit option. They need superior alternatives to be demonstrated, advertised, and offered them.

So given the analysis here, Breneman(1983) and *The Economist*(1992) author also appear to be half right. Voice is important as emphasized. But it causes negative not positive externalities. The existence of the pushing, prodding parents of high-aptitude pupils causes inequality. This leads to *dynamic inefficiency* and encourages parents to spend their time in zero-sum, rent-seeking behavior.

Note

1   National Center For Education Statistics; U.S. Department of Education,
    Digest of Edcuation Statistics(1993) table 240, p. 249.

Chapter IX

A Superior Common
School Policy: Vouchers

Many of the important determinants for educational quality have been isolated using the theory of learning capital and the *High School and Beyond* Data. The empirical evidence indicates that some schools are organized in a manner that leads to common school excellence. Some schools are not organized as well. The distinguishing factor for how well a school is organized is whether the school is public or private. Unfortunately, most pupils in the United States are enrolled in the inferior public schools.

If the United States is to live up to the educational ideals contained within the common school philosophy, then a policy change is required. Given the superiority of private schools on the common school criteria and the damaging effect of the voice mechanism in democratically-controlled schools, a policy of regulated competition should be adopted. As evident, a decentralized, free-enterprise system of education is more creative and thus more effective in transforming educational resources into intellectual growth, equality, and integration. If the state is determined to protect an industry from the insecurities and anxieties of competition, perhaps it should be in autos, not education. Costly and unreliable cars are preferred to defective and costly children.

This proposed policy of school competition should be placed within the context of a general educational policy. Neither an extreme laissez-faire educational policy nor a state monopoly is wise. For reasons of allocative efficiency and justice, the state should finance primary and secondary education through taxation. For reasons of minority, socio-economic, and handicap integration; the state should legislate minimum integration levels. For the purpose of promoting a common American Culture, the state should define a minimum core-curricula. For reasons of equality, *c-efficiency*, *selection efficiency*, and *dynamic efficiency*; the private sector should supply primary and secondary education. So regulated competition through the use of vouchers, financed through taxation is the recommended common school policy.

With the common school criteria as the goals, an effective voucher policy would have several characteristics. First, it has to be implemented on a regional level such as a city or state. Democratically-elected representatives would define the minimum integration standards for each social category within each school. Obviously, this would depend on the characteristics of the general student population in the vicinity of the schools. The standards must also be set with full knowledge of the tradeoff between integration and efficiency. The state would also define the minimum curriculum requirements for content of study such as civics. Schools that do not satisfy minimum integration and core-curriculum requirements are denied participation in the scholarship program.

Second, each pupil's voucher or scholarship should be redeemable and transferable on a yearly basis at most. If students could transfer schools on a semester or quarterly basis, efficiency would increase because aggregate instructional error would decrease. The more frequent the student trades permitted, the lower is σ at the beginning of each instructional period; and thus the more *selection efficiency* achieved.

Third, for each student cohort, a pupil's scholarship should be *negatively* related to the pupil's aptitude. This would be comparable to the traditional understanding of vertical equity since aptitude is positively related to family income. This formula encourages the instructional target(V^*) within each school to be targeted toward the lowest aptitude pupils which eventually causes more equality and more *dynamic efficiency* for each and every school. The opportunity cost of losing a lower-aptitude pupil through exit would be larger than for a higher-aptitude pupil. Therefore, lower-aptitude pupils would attract more optimum instructional targets and thus enjoy higher learning rates within every school. This element of the policy would also result in the schools having the lower mean aptitude levels to enjoy progressively larger mean values for e_i. This funding premium and the corresponding higher teacher salaries would encourage teachers to forfeit the intellectual prestige of teaching at high aptitude levels as well as encourage them to work with the more disagreeable pupils.

The negative gradient between aptitudes and the scholarships should not be steep. There is already a natural, or built-in bias toward the low-achiever even with equal scholarships if the school is to be *dynamically efficient*. The steeper the gradient the more the policy becomes politically unacceptable to middle and higher-aptitude pupil/families. It would also cause an incentive problem since the more a pupil learns the lower his scholarship. Perhaps the state or a private firm could implement standardized tests at the end of each school year. The results of these tests could then be sent to the private schools pursuing an efficient enrollment policy. Also, using these test results for the purpose of awarding the scholarships would discourage students from deliberately scoring low for the purpose of keeping their scholarships high. This dishonest behavior would cause them to be placed in a school with too low an instructional target and thus suffer a lower rate of learning.

Finally, most voucher proposals forbid families from adding on to their scholarship value with personal expenditures(Coons and Sugarman, 1975; Chubb and Moe, 1990). The fear is that children from wealthy families who spend treasures would accelerate intellectually beyond all other students and produce unacceptable inequalities. However, this rationale for forbidding add-ons is based on exaggerated effects of funding as well as other faulty reasoning. The recommendation here is to permit add-ons for several reasons.

First, there are dramatically diminishing returns to cognitive growth from funding as evident in regression one and Hanushek's(1986, 1989) review articles. In fact, partly due to the current high spending-level in many schools, there is a zero marginal impact on cognitive growth from higher e_i. Hence, more spending merely results in more school luxury goods which have no impact on the level of learning capital(K_j). The idea that high intelligence growth can be instantaneously purchased with sufficient expenditures is an exaggeration. The production of intellectual growth quickly becomes a time-intensive, not a money-intensive commodity. In fact, time is most expensive for children from wealthy families who are encouraged to live activity-filled days. No doubt, wealthy families can use their wealth in a manner that "purchases" time-on-task(T_i) for their children. But this behavior occurs whether add-ons are permitted or not. The point is that marginal increases in the rate of learning due to increases in e_i within a school approaches zero as e_i increases.

The second reason add-ons should be permitted is because with more total funding in the system more schools can be opened. The more schools that can reach the critical mass in funding, the more V^*'s available in a geographic region which all students can choose from and thus maximize their learning rates. If higher-aptitude pupils from wealthy families can afford to open their own school they are not in a larger school competing for the scarce teacher attention and scarce instructional targets. Also, even if a few families spend large sums of money at one school, the resources still become "public property" within the school. So a large add-on becomes a subsidy for many. Regression twenty provides evidence that marginal increases in e_i is targeted toward lower-achievers within a school.

Finally, permitting add-ons would make the entire plan more politically acceptable due to the negative relationship between the scholarship and aptitude as proposed above. It would also satisfy allocational efficiency criteria by recognizing differential tastes for education. As a final comment, policymakers trying to encourage culture and intellectual development would be foolish to deliberately constrain spending to more private luxury goods instead of more education.

Chapter X

Conclusion

If the policy of regulated competition is enacted the educational system is expected to become more efficient and more equal. Also, the quality of the Nation's general economy is intimately connected to the quality of its educational system. If education improves, the efficiency and equity properties of the general economy should improve. Some general comments are now offered concerning the benefits of having a competitive school system.

10.1 Smarter Graduates

The first common school goal was to maximize cognitive achievement growth(q_i) given the financial(e_i) and time-on-task(T_i) constraints. A more developed intellect leads to a more productive worker, wiser consumer, and more responsible citizen. To see how intellectual growth is furthered with competition, the theoretical model(4.1) is re-visited below. With competition the expression in brackets is expected to increase while e_i and T_i are theoretically held constant. As a result, q_i increases during any instructional period. Increasing the bracketed expression is precisely how schools are expected to attract pupil/families and thus avoid financial bankruptcy.

The behavior of private schools shows this to be the case even with the small amount of competition present when the *High School and Beyond* Sample was drawn.

(from 4.1) $$\frac{q_i}{e_i} = \left\{ \frac{\theta_i N}{c + \beta \|V_i - V^*\|} \right\} T_i$$

Specifically, c is expected to decrease since administrators would be constrained to allocate their spending for inputs that have the highest marginal product per-dollar for the production of K* within each student's track. Hence, bureaucratic positions unrelated to the production of learning capital would be discouraged and teacher competence and communication skill would be encouraged and rewarded. Teacher experience would also receive relatively more weight in salary schedules compared to beginning salary and graduate degrees as evident from regression six.

The expected level for the instructional error expression in the denominator would also decrease. Schools would have an incentive to be pareto-optimal in their setting of V*. So the possibility of having redundant or overwhelming textbooks and lectures for every pupil in a class would be minimized. Hence, competition would purge unnecessary redundancy and confusion. And of course, the instructional error expression is expected to be further minimized by minimizing σ and $\Delta\sigma$ so that the average value for θ_i in the numerator can remain high. Ability-tracking within a school would also be reduced since it is an inefficient as well as unequal method for minimizing instructional error.

There are two additional sources of efficiency enhancement that might occur. If the bracketed expression in 4.1 becomes larger, each student's learning rate increases. If pupils' study-time becomes more fruitful in cognitive growth, their attention spans might expand which might cause them to become more committed scholars. Hence, schools' resources would be more fully utilized by raising the reward for a pupil's perseverance in time-on-task(Carroll, 1963; McKenzie and Staaf, 1974; Davisson and Bonello, 1976; Bloom, 1976). For instance, private schools are characterized by higher levels of time-on-task(T_i)(table 5.2), perhaps partly due to their higher learning rates. Children are like adults; they become restless when they sense their time is being wasted.

Finally, public school districts today are characterized by large inequalities in expenditures per-pupil(e_i) due mainly to differential property tax bases. The policy proposed above could result in more equal expenditures per-pupil(e_i) across schools if add-ons are not sufficiently high to counteract the negative scholarship-aptitude gradient. This would have the effect of raising the average K_i and thus q_i in the entire school system. Why would more equality in expenditures per-pupil(e_i) lead to a higher mean learning rate for the entire school system? Again, there exists diminishing returns to funding which means that taking a dollar from a high-spending school and re-allocating it to a lower-spending school raises the average learning rate between the two schools(Johnson and Stafford, 1973). Luxury expenditures irrelevant to the production of learning capital in the affluent school are converted into learning capital necessities in the low-spending school.

10.2 *More Equality Within and Between Schools*

Education is important to economists because cognitive abilities largely determine one's wage or salary opportunities due to the concept of human capital(Mincer, 1958; Shultz, 1963; Becker, 1975; Blaug, 1976, 1987). The more competent an employee, the larger his marginal productivity in producing a firm's output. So if more education leads to higher income for the individual, then production of more equality in education should result in more income equality. Or, the production and distribution of learning capital ultimately determines a society's aggregate income and its distribution due to the intervening formation of human capital.

An important question is how the proposed policy of school competition might influence the distribution of income in the United States as a whole. It is believed income distribution would become more equal. To see this, two types of equality have to be distinguished. First, $\Delta\sigma$ measures the extent of achievement inequality produced within the typical school. As discussed previously, this is expected to decrease insofar as schools compete on grounds of *dynamic efficiency*. As a result, income opportunities between graduates within a given school in a particular geographic region should become more equal on graduation day since their final achievement levels will be more equal.

The second type of achievement equality has not been discussed. Each school can be distinguished by the average q_i it indirectly produces for its student body by directly producing an average K_i. The second type of equality measures the dispersion of mean q_i *between* all schools in the United States. Will the voucher policy promote more equality *between* schools? Or will it exacerbate inequality?

To answer this, notice from the average characteristics of schools in table 5.2 that private schools attract students with relatively higher initial cognitive achievement as measured by sophomore test scores(s_1). Notice further that private schools produce the most cognitive growth(q_i) on the average for their student bodies over the two year instructional period. Hence, the cumulative effect of the current educational structure is to exacerbate the inequality of final average achievement between schools. Not only do private schools start with the highest achievers, they also facilitate a faster growth rate for them. So the hybrid system of efficient private schools starting with high-achievers and inefficient public schools starting with low-achievers leads to more inequality in the final stock of achievement for every graduating cohort. Students in the upper tail grow faster intellectually than students in the lower-aptitude tail; not because of natural abilities, but because of the efficiency of their respective schools.

To the extent the frequency or concentration of middle-aptitudes is reduced from this process, the middle-aptitude class becomes less prevalent. Over time, the smart grow smarter while the ignorant grow *relatively* more ignorant. Or because of the positive linkage between aptitude and the wage rate; the rich grow richer, the poor grow relatively poorer. Again, this is due to private schools starting at a higher achievement level and then proceeding faster. Within public schools, intellectual growth is dispersed and thus stunted on the average. Within private schools, it is compacted and thus accelerated on the average. So the dwindling middle-income class in the United States is partially attributed to the dwindling middle-aptitude class caused by the cumulative impact of the present educational package. Without school competition, the United States has produced and will continue to produce a culture that is bifurcated intellectually and economically.

The important point is that a voucher policy would improve both within-school and between-school equality of final achievement. If public schools imitated the efficient private schools by lowering their values for σ and $\Delta\sigma$, then the gap or range between the upper and lower achievement and income quartiles within the United States would decrease. This is especially true since voucher values are negatively related to average aptitude levels between schools. Finally, if income equality improves over time, then the future cost of integrating different socio-economic classes would decrease since the dispersion of the socio-economic status between families within the United States would also be minimized. Also, a more equal primary and secondary education system would emit positive externalities on universities searching for minimum aptitude dispersion in order to enhance their own *selection efficiency*.

10.3 Upward Mobility?

In addition to the three common school goals of productive efficiency, equality of opportunity, and integration; there is a fourth criterion for evaluating a school system. What is the likelihood of having an Horatio Alger success story in the present public-school system? Or what are the chances of an initially low-aptitude child from an immigrant, low-income family to excel intellectually to the top of his national cohort? The child cannot do this alone by merely putting in heroic levels of time-on-task(T_i). The child needs guidance, direction, explanation, encouragement, and prodding on a daily basis. In other words, the child needs quality instruction or a high K_i throughout if high levels of effort are to pay off. To enjoy a high K_i, the child must have a consistently optimal instructional target throughout each instructional period. For instance, instruction on Thursday morning must pick up where the student left off Wednesday night.

The possibility for upward mobility in the present system of public education appears to be minimal. To see this, suppose Horatio, the pupil, is currently in the general track at a public high school. He has put in sufficiently high T_i to have a higher aptitude than his peers in the general track who do not study as much. Since instruction is targeted toward his lower-aptitude peers, he is experiencing positive instructional error. In other words, V_i is greater than V^* in the general track and therefore his learning rate(K_i) is currently quite low.

His options for obtaining a more optimal $V*$ and thus higher learning rate are limited. The academic track within his high school has a higher $V*$, but it is too high and thus overwhelming for his current aptitude. So within the academic track V_i is less than $V*$ for Horatio. Neither the general nor the academic track satisfies his unique needs.

His own efforts in T_i are unlikely to deliver him to the aptitude level of the academic track within his present high school. For even a maximum level of T_i is insufficient to legitimately remediate himself into the academic track because his K_i is too low to produce a sufficiently high $q_i(q_i = K_iT_i)$. He is also chasing an aptitude or instructional target that is moving further away from his own aptitude over time. His family does not have the resources to provide sufficiently intense family or private tutoring to facilitate the discreet jump between tracks.[1] Horatio's high school administrator cannot adjust $V*$ to satisfy his unique instructional needs because that would merely hurt his peers if resources are taken from them. State law discourages him from transferring to another public school that might have a more optimal $V*$. His parents do not have the funds to enroll him in a private school with a more optimal $V*$. The result is for Horatio to adopt the intellectual standards of the general track with a lower and slower moving $V*$. His initial low-aptitude, low family income position influenced his subsequent intellectual advancement more than Horatio's desire and effort.

Are these mere excuses for Horatio's low achievement or is he a casualty of an educational policy that has the effect of violating the spirit of the common school philosophy? Educational policy makers should desire to enhance the possibility for Horatio's upward mobility. A competitive school system would reduce the obstacles to Horatio's advancement. Having too few instructional targets($V*$) for pupil/ families to choose from is one of the central constraints to upward mobility in the present system. To see this, suppose there are N pupils residing in a county who are distributed among several schools. The average level of instructional error in this county is μ_c(10.1):

$$(10.1) \quad \mu_c = \frac{\beta}{N} \sum_{i=1}^{N} \| V_i - V* \|$$

where:

μ_c = county-wide average instructional error.
V_i = ith pupil's aptitude vector.
V^* = instructional target within ith pupil's track within ith pupil's school.

Upward mobility as well as overall productive efficiency is enhanced within the county the larger the number of *unique* V^*'s distributed throughout the aptitude space. The supply of unique V^*'s should increase with competition since schools would compete by offering unique V^*'s. For example, a population of Asian-Americans might need a curriculum of remedial English and advanced science both initially taught in their native language. Whereas white Americans might require a curriculum of advanced English, intermediate science, and perhaps a foreign language all taught in English. Each student can then use their personal T_i to move between the instructional targets of schools. The more V^*'s, the less burden placed on student's own heroic levels of time-on-task(T_i) or expensive private tutoring in the pursuit of more learning. However, in the present system, too many instructional targets are duplicated by geographically-adjacent schools. The point is that the finer the gradations between V^*'s the larger the opportunity for student effort to pay off in upward mobility throughout the entire system.

This barrier to upward mobility can also be analyzed by examining differential norms for time-on-task(T_i) rather than mere raw instructional error. Suppose two geographically-adjacent schools begin a school year with identical curriculums or instructional targets. So for the purpose of minimal instructional error during the initial instructional period, Horatio might be indifferent between these two schools. However, in one school V^* progresses more rapidly since academic expectations or the average level of homework(T_i) the teacher is able to elicit from students is greater. Having the choice between these two schools prevents the mediocre learning standards of Horatio's neighborhood school being the final arbiter of his educational lot in life. John Carroll(1989, p. 30) has argued similarly in the context of what public schools should provide:

Equality of opportunity to attain potentials implies that students with different amounts and kinds of aptitude need to have educational programs that differ in pace and content, and perhaps in many other ways. As someone has put it, we need not only equality of opportunity but also diversity of opportunity.

So in the present system it is uncertain whether Horatio's underachiever status is due to arbitrarily low academic standards being imposed upon him by his teachers and/or his peers or whether it is due to Horatio and his family being indifferent or careless. In a free enterprise system of education, characterized by a competitive supply of both instructional targets(V^*) and norms for time-on-task(T_i), policy makers could be more confident that motivation to learn more is greeted with opportunity to learn more. At the same time, pupils with less motivation for school learning would still enjoy maximum learning rates during their lower levels of time-on-task.

10.4 More Money For Education

Economists are the pariahs among educational analysts. Their inclination is to cut or stall the growth rate of educational budgets since the marginal product of funding has approached zero. However, the increase of educational budgets can be both predicted and defended using economic theory provided that vouchers are adopted. It is believed the democratic-election process in any political jurisdiction adopting vouchers would be expected to result in higher expenditures per-pupil(e_i). In other words, the median voter/taxpayer would desire a larger commitment of a state's budget for educational expenditures per-pupil(e_i). Why might this be?

Again, the bracketed expression in equation 4.1 is expected to increase with competition. In other words, the cost per-unit of learning capital(e_i/K_i = inverse of the bracketed expression) should decrease due to σ and $\Delta\sigma$ being lower. The optimal level of e_i should rise for the median voter due both to the substitution and income effects of standard consumer theory. First, the median voter would desire to transfer expenditures towards the relatively cheaper good of learning capital(K_i) that has both consumption and investment properties. There would also be a "production-oriented" substitution effect toward higher educational spending. For it would be optimal for parents to finance a substitution away from T_i or time-on-task toward a higher K_i through more e_i. Families are just like firms in that they will use relatively more of the cheaper input for cognitive production. When the bracketed expression in 4.1 increases, the input K_i becomes a relatively cheaper input relative to the time-on-task(T_i) input($q_i = K_i T_i$).

The income effect is expected to operate in the same positive direction and thus increase e_i. As the price per-unit of learning capital falls(e_i/K_i), the income effect should be positive since education is a normal good. Also, if a higher mean q_i results from more efficient schools, then the median level of human capital increases. In the long run, this inevitably increases the median disposable income which should further cause an expansion in the desired amount of learning capital(K_i). Finally, if competition is implemented, then more taxes for the purpose of increased educational spending would become an attractive political platform.

10.5 *Dissipating the Costs of Integration*

One finding of this work is that there exists opportunity costs in integrating a school with respect to race, ethnicity, and socio-economic status. Different cultures emphasize intellectual development differently and thus have different historical educations and thus different present aptitudes. No doubt, some of these differences are also due to previously unequal levels of learning capital due to persistent instructional error. Nevertheless, to the extent these different learning cultures are combined in a single school, the dispersion of aptitudes increases which decreases the school's efficiency.

If the voucher policy is implemented, the marginal cost of integration should decrease over time. Why might this occur? Again, each school is required to satisfy minimum integration requirements which decreases *selection efficiency* by raising σ at the beginning of each instructional period. However, in order to be *dynamically efficient*, the school will initially target these integrated, disadvantaged students intensively in order to minimize aptitude dispersion over time. In other words, the combination of integration requirements and the efficiency property of homogeneous aptitudes causes premiums to be placed on minority and low-income students who also have high aptitudes. Since this type of student is rare in the general population but is nevertheless a relatively high valued student, the school has an incentive to "produce" this type of student. This is especially true for schools with higher mean aptitudes.

Since this policy encourages school administrators to "produce" more high-aptitude students from historically lower-educated social groups, there should be an increasing proportion of them over time. Hence, the aptitude levels of these historically disadvantaged groups are remediated and become increasingly similar to the distribution of aptitudes in the general population over time. As a result, enrolling minorities and lower socio-economic students no longer involves as significant an increase in σ and $\Delta\sigma$ as before. Therefore, as social integration is expanded within a school the mean level for K_i/e_i or q_i/e_i does not decrease as much. There is a decreased necessity to implement remedial or accelerated tracks upon social integration. Hence, the marginal cost of integration decreases. In conclusion, the marginal cost of integration is not likely to be eliminated but it should decrease and be maintained at a lower level.

10.6 Teacher Labor Market

Teacher unions have previously opposed voucher proposals. Obviously, no worker in any industry would appreciate the anxieties and uncertainties that accompany a disruption of one's livelihood. But to review, teachers should find several expected outcomes attractive. Having more homogeneous aptitudes in a school should increase the intellectual rewards of teaching. Second, education would be expected to be better funded which would increase salaries as will be seen below. Finally, Lee, Dedrick, and Smith(1991) and Bryk, Lee, and Holland(1993) offer evidence that teachers in Catholic schools are more satisfied with their jobs relative to public school teachers despite the lower pay. Lee, Dedrick, and Smith(1991) conclude that "Staff collegiality(communal organization, staff influence in decision-making, collaboration time, and knowledge of others' courses) is stronger in Catholic schools. Teachers in Catholic schools are also higher on ratings of leadership(principal leadership, encouraging innovation, administrative responsiveness)."

Because teacher support would be vital for a successful voucher policy, it is useful to speculate on the factors that might influence teacher demand under the proposed policy. Teacher demand is a derived demand that follows from the consumers' demand for learning capital(K_i). Pupil/families are attracted to a school where the teaching staff produces a high learning rate in each of the academic subjects. Along with the pupil/families comes revenue from their respective scholarships. So as a crude approximation, the marginal revenue product for a teacher's service might be calculated as 10.2 below. The expression demonstrates that teachers are demanded or evaluated with respect to their marginal contribution toward a high learning rate(K^*) for the targeted student within their assigned track. This teaching skill ultimately attracts students(N) and thus revenue(e).

$$(10.2) \quad \frac{\partial N}{\partial K^*} \; \frac{\partial K^*}{\partial X} \; e \; = \; \text{salary}$$

where:

N = student enrollment in school
K^* = rate of learning for targeted student within track
X = hours of service by the teacher hired
e = average scholarship value among the marginal student enrollment attracted by the contracting of services X.

Analyzing the marginal revenue product(10.2) in more detail suggests several properties concerning teacher demand and corresponding equilibrium salaries. First, there seems to be a fear that teachers' skill could be artificially inflated if they merely had harder working students. But in the context of the theory of learning capital, a teacher's salary is independent or unrelated to their students' time-on-task(T_i). Teachers are paid by their contribution to a learning rate, not the more intrusive act of getting students to sacrifice their part-time work or leisure-time activities. Again, the norms for time-on-task(T_i) partly established by the teacher are important and relevant to the pupil/family. But whether pupils are benefiting from *any* level of time-on-task(T_i) is the more important prior question. Bloom(1968, p. 84) concurs with this reasoning:

There seems to be little reason to make learning so difficult that only a small proportion of the students can persevere to mastery. Endurance and unusual perseverance may be appropriate for long-distance running - they are not great virtues in their own right. The emphasis should be on learning, not on vague ideas of discipline and endurance.

It is also a fallacy that teachers would merely look good and therefore get paid more if they attracted the initially higher-achievers or high-aptitude pupils. The rate of learning is independent of the initial intellectual position of students. Even more, salaries are negatively related to student aptitude. This is because e or the average scholarship of the marginal group of students that the teacher attracts is negatively related to their mean aptitude by policy design. Hence, the teachers that are more talented at maximizing the learning rate for lower-aptitude students are paid more. However, if both scholarship add-ons and the number of pupil/families adding-on were sufficiently high, then this conclusion is reversed.

Third, a teacher's salary increases with respect to the quantity of students(N) the teacher attracts. This is perhaps necessary since more students would likely involve more effort for the teacher. Finally and more important, teachers with more academic competence and communication skill would be characterized by a larger marginal product for K* within their subject of expertise. The more intelligible the lectures and reading material, the higher the teacher demand and thus salary.

Finally, administrators' compensation would be proportional to their performance in minimizing expected instructional error through their enrollment policy and overall curriculum design, hiring and retaining effective teachers, and providing for an orderly learning environment. All these labor market properties appear reasonably fair *if* there is to be a positive association between merit and salary.

10.7 Obfuscating the School Question

In order to compare public and private schools, expected values for q_i/e_i were calculated for each sector given their respective average values for σ and $\Delta\sigma$. In order to be sensitive to significant differences for policy purposes, the raw difference for mean q_i/e_i between public and private schools was converted into a proportional difference. The typical private school was found to be 14.81% more efficient. Other analysts of the *High School and Beyond* Data believe that a simple proportion like this is inadequate and that a more sophisticated and thus superior measure exists for assessing a relevant sector difference. However, it is argued that their measure is flawed; for it is incapable of measuring *any* of the common school benefits stemming from competition.

Coleman, Hoffer, and Greeley(1985), Willms(1985), and Alexander and Pallas(1985) use q_i as their dependent variable while controlling for family influences and student "ability" when testing for a sector difference. Again, they ignore expenditures and any corresponding discussion of efficiency. They also do not control for time-on-task(T_i) which was assumed to be a policy variable within the school and thus should be allowed to distinguish sector quality. Hence, more time-on-task(T_i) was unambiguously better even if learning rates(K_i) were low. Also, generally speaking, they used fewer family, community, and school control variables than were used in this work. Thus, their respective measures for sector differences were more liberal in favor of the Catholic sector.

Using the Catholic sector dummy variable from their regressions, each researcher was able to calculate the expected gap between public and private cognitive growth(q_i) for the typical student while controlling for non-school factors. For interpretation purposes; Coleman, Hoffer, and Greeley(1985) used measure 10.3 to standardize and interpret the average difference between a Catholic and public school. It is the Catholic sector advantage in cognitive growth expressed as a percentage of public-sector cognitive growth. So public sector growth is the norm for sector comparison. Notice that the numerator in 10.3 can also be interpreted as the parameter for the Catholic sector dummy variable.

$$(10.3) \quad \% \text{ Catholic advantage} \quad = \quad \frac{q_c - q_p}{q_p}$$

where:

q_c = expected cognitive growth in Catholic sector for typical student over the final two years of high school.

q_p = expected cognitive growth in public sector for typical student over final the two years of high school.

Using 10.3, Coleman, Hoffer, and Greeley(1985) found the Catholic advantage to be approximately 35.6% during the last two years of high school which they interpreted as significantly large. As a result, Coleman, Hoffer, and Greeley(1985, p. 96) concluded that "the greater effectiveness of the Catholic schools, which must compete, against strong economic odds, for students, suggests that a little competition might not be harmful for American public schools."

Willms(1985) and Alexander and Pallas(1985) reject Coleman, Hoffer, and Greeley's(1985) proportional measure(10.3) as well as their corresponding policy recommendation. They prefer expression 10.4 to measure the output differential between a Catholic and a public school. It is the Catholic advantage expressed as a percentage of the standard deviation of senior test scores for all pupils in the *High School and Beyond* Sample. Using 10.4, Alexander and Pallas(1985, p. 121) found the sector gap to be approximately 6.3% of a standard deviation. Whereas, Willms(1985, p. 112) calculated it for each individual test and found the largest Catholic advantage on one test to be approximately 6.9%.

$$(10.4) \quad \% \text{ Catholic advantage} = \frac{q_c - q_p}{\sigma_{pooled}}$$

where:

σ_{pooled} = pooled standard deviation of senior test scores for all students, both public and Catholic.

So placing the pooled standard deviation in the denominator makes a significant difference in measuring the sector difference. It seems to significantly lower the Catholic advantage. Willms(1985) and Alexander and Pallas(1985) believe their measure superior to the simple proportion(10.3) employed by Coleman, Hoffer and Greeley(1985):

> it facilitates comparisons of estimates of Catholic-school effects found in this study with those observed in earlier studies...Second, it is the most informative and straightforward measure of an experimental effect size...and can take on added meaning when referred to the effects of well-known interventions...Third, the standardization makes no assumption about the amount of growth that is due to

school factors, as opposed to nonschool factors(Willms; 1985, p.111).

> These comparisons allow us to judge the average test-score difference across sectors against the variability in the trait. This seems to us to be the best of the less-than-ideal options that are available...(Alexander and Pallas; 1985, p. 121).

To their credit, Willms(1985) and Alexander and Pallas'(1985) measure does reveal that a public-school pupil would not improve her position dramatically relative to the overall distribution of cognitive abilities by being placed in a Catholic school. However, this is an argument to abolish schooling in the last two years of high school not a comparison of sector performance. Is it not a "red herring" to change the research question in the middle of the analysis from 'Is there a sector difference?' to 'How important is schooling during the final two years of high school in altering a pupil's relative position?' For as a proportion of what formal education can accomplish within the public sector, the Catholic sector appears superior.

Nevertheless, based on the lower proportions that result from using their preferred measure(10.4); Willms(1985) and Alexander and Pallas(1985) conclude that there is no policy-significant difference in cognitive growth between the Catholic and public sectors:

> policy decisions should not be based on the assumption that either public or private schools produce better achievement outcomes... this study, which is based on a longitudinal analysis of growth in student achievement, finds no substantial differences between comparable students in the public and private sectors(Willms; 1985, p. 113).

> We judge differences of this magnitude to be substantively trivial... These sector effects simply do not matter much, and talking about them as though they do is both poor science and a poor basis for informing public policy(Alexander and Pallas; 1985, p. 115 and 125).

Since the researchers read each others' manuscripts prior to publication, they were able to dialogue concerning methods and interpretation. Thus, Coleman, Hoffer, and Greeley(1985) criticize Willms(1985) and Alexander and Pallas'(1985) proportional measure(10.4) and corresponding policy conclusions:

The results we have shown make it difficult to believe that the impact of Catholic school on sophomore-to-senior achievement growth is no greater or only trivially greater than that of the average public school... if one concludes that these differences in growth are trivial, one must also conclude that the growth in achievement in the last two years of high school is trivial...(Coleman, Hoffer, and Greeley; 1985, p. 96)

American educators and educational researchers typically assume that Catholic schools are academically inferior to public schools. They attribute this inferiority to larger classes, less-professional teacher training, more limited resources, smaller per-pupil costs, and religious narrowness, which they believe restricts thought and imagination. To show that Catholic schools, for all their apparent weaknesses, are not worse than public schools may not be too unsettling. But to suggest, as we have, that in terms of academic outcome they might be somewhat better is such a reversal of conventional wisdom that one might well expect intense debate(Coleman, Hoffer, and Greeley; 1985, p. 96).

So from the perspective of the learning capital theory, which method and corresponding conclusion is correct? Even though Coleman, Hoffer, and Greeley's(1985) method is weak due to omitting the opportunity costs of money and time as well as ignoring instructional error; their method and corresponding conclusions are more accurate. Why is Willm's(1985) and Alexander and Pallas'(1985) measure flawed?

First, the pooled standard deviation of test scores appearing in the denominator of 10.4 is dependent on school policy due to the preceding evidence on each school's value for $\Delta\sigma$(regressions 14 through 20). Intra-school resource allocation(θ_i and V^*) eventually determines the senior year dispersion of test scores within each school as well as the *dynamic efficiency* of each school. Pooling or adding together all of the schools' respective dispersions does not change this fact. Thus, Willms'(1985, p.111) assertion that the pooled standard deviation is neutral to "school factors" is inappropriate.

Second and more important, their measure is incapable of measuring relative sector quality based on the common school criteria. In fact, it is both possible and probable for the relative efficiency and equality of the Catholic sector to improve over time, while their measure would detect relative deterioration within the Catholic sector.

To see this, suppose the average level for $\Delta\sigma$ increases within the public sector while the average Catholic value remains constant. Hence, the public sector's performance in equality and *dynamic efficiency* decreased compared to the Catholic sector. Further assume that the public school budget(e_i) expanded sufficiently to compensate for this efficiency decrease so that expected cognitive growth for the public sector(q_p) remained constant in the numerator of 10.4. The public schools may have used the additional funding to add aptitude-tracks to accommodate the higher dispersion of aptitudes and thus maintain q_p at a constant level.

Given this realistic scenario, how does Willms'(1985) and Alexander and Pallas'(1985) proportional measure(10.4) change? The numerator remains constant. Both the Catholic and public schools' expected values for q_i are the same. The denominator increases due to the larger public sector values for $\Delta\sigma$ during the last two years of high school. So the Catholic advantage expressed as a fraction of the pooled standard deviation of senior test scores decreased. As a result, the measured Catholic advantage over the public sector has decreased when in fact it increased. Or similarly, when the typical public school becomes more unequal and more inefficient, Willms'(1985) and Alexander and Pallas'(1985) proportional measure(10.4) registers a public sector relative improvement. So using their measure, the public sector cannot lose! The public sector's relative performance appears to improve when they become more unequal and less *dynamically efficient*.

To summarize, the problem with Willms'(1985) and Alexander and Pallas'(1985) measurement is twofold. First, when designing the measure they ignore the fact that the pooled standard deviation of senior test scores is quite sensitive to the specific school policy of intra-school allocation of resources(θ_i and V^*). In other words, the dispersion of aptitudes at the end of a schooling period is just as important an output as the average q_i. It has both intrinsic and instrumental importance. This leads to the second problem with the measure. It is not acknowledged that a causal relationship exists between the denominator and the numerator. Or that σ and $\Delta\sigma$ determines the expected level of q_i for each sector in the numerator, given each school's fixed budget.

A final comment is necessary concerning Willms'(1985) and Alexander and Pallas'(1985) conclusion that placing a public-school pupil into a Catholic school would not significantly improve the pupil's relative position in her age cohort. This conclusion appears to be correct. But the reason Catholic schooling is ineffective in raising the pupil's relative position in the *overall* dispersion of final achievement within the cohort is because public schools have produced too large a dispersion. In conclusion, the pooled standard deviation of senior test scores in the denominator does not "standardize" the experimental effect as argued by Willms(1985) and Alexander and Pallas(1985). It conceals and obfuscates it.

10.8 Weaknesses of the Theory of Learning Capital

Approaching the school question from the perspective of instructional error and learning capital has been insightful because the inter-connections of efficiency, equality, and integration has been demonstrated. However, many important educational questions remain unanswered and cannot be answered using the theory of learning capital. A few of these issues are now surveyed.

The theory of learning capital analyzes the forces that lead to high intellectual growth. The question of what subjects should be studied given that one cannot study all of them even in a lifetime is not addressed. For example, should there be a foreign language requirement? Which periods of history should be emphasized? What is the appropriate mix between vocational and academic courses? Should ethics be included in the existing curriculum, ignored, or studied in a separate course? What should be the relative weight between learning facts and developing analytic and evaluative skills?

These are questions that must be debated and answered if a policy of vouchers accompanied with a core-curriculum requirement should ever be implemented. For the consumer model breaks down on this issue. By definition, students and perhaps some parents are un-informed with respect to what they should study. For if students knew what was intellectually best for them, they most likely would no longer be pupils in need of instruction. The whole idea of education rests on the premise that an information gap or expertise gap exists between the consumer and supplier. The pupil/family places a degree of trust on the educator's wisdom in providing a quality curriculum. There is a potential for a consensus on a core-curriculum; for educational analysts agreed on a battery of test questions for the *High School and Beyond* Survey for the purpose of comparing sector quality.

Related to this question is the issue of studying religion in schools, especially private schools. Would it be a violation of the establishment clause of the first amendment of the Constitution if vouchers indirectly funded the practice and study of different religions? If government funds were distributed to religiously-affiliated schools, what proportion would be used for liturgical activity and the hiring of religious teachers and purchase of religious texts? No doubt, there would be some. For example, students in Catholic schools spend part of their school week attending mass and studying theology. The legal question of the separation of church and state was ignored here.

However, those defending the present public-school system using this Constitutional reasoning must adopt an uncomfortable corollary position. To the extent religious schools presently dedicate school-time and money toward the study and practice of their religions, time-on-task(T_i) and financial resources(e_i) are taken from the study of secular subjects. If students in these religious schools are still able to learn more in the secular subjects compared to their public school counterparts, then the religious schools are even more efficient compared to public schools than what has been estimated here. In other words, the more resources found to be dedicated to religious activities within these schools, the better the church schools are at teaching the secular subjects.

Third, three types of school efficiency were defined here: *c-efficiency*, *selection efficiency*, and *dynamic efficiency*. The theoretical and policy analyses proceeded as if a comprehensive evaluation was performed across sectors for every efficiency category. However, only *dynamic* and *selection efficiency* were analyzed due to data limitations as well as the ambiguity of assigning school responsibility to some of the *c-efficiency* variables. So the question of sector performance in *c-efficiency* remains unanswered. However, there exists a large presumption against the public sector for this category due to the *costs* of their large above-high-school bureaucracies being omitted while the *effect* or *benefit* of their services being included.

Fourth, to keep this research in perspective, it must be remembered that the *High School and Beyond* Data provided only a portrait of secondary education during the academic years 1981 and 1982. Relative sector performance could vary by grade levels. This analysis ignored sector performance from kindergarten through tenth grade. Also, sector behavior could have changed in the years since the survey was taken. However, there seems to be no obvious reason why public and private sector behavior would be different in either case.

Finally, voucher programs have been criticized on the grounds that pupil/families simply could not make a rational choice on which school to attend. This may be the case if schools offered different subject-oriented curriculums as discussed above. However, if a core-curriculum is mandated across schools, this is not a persuasive critique of vouchers. The underlying assumption of the critique inevitably becomes: Pupil/families cannot distinguish between a productively efficient school from an inefficient school. In other words, they would be un-informed concerning the pedagogical determinants of effective learning for their child. This critique would be valid only if the experts knew better. But after reviewing the results of 187 educational production function studies, even the theoreticians and empirical analysts equipped with regression techniques have been dumfounded on this question.

Given the theory of learning capital, pupil/families need not be infinitely wise and rational concerning educational production. The pupil/family merely chooses one of several schools that seems to minimize redundancy and/or confusion when learning how to read, write, and calculate. Pupil/parents could attend sample lectures, review textbooks, and discuss homework requirements with teachers and administrators. They need not articulate the theory of instructional error nor be familiar with regression results. In fact, pupil/families may be superior at detecting the presence of instructional error since it depends on their personal and complex aptitude vector which is imperfectly measured using aptitude tests. Parents might also be the best judge on what can reasonably be expected from the pupil-child in perseverance on homework.

10.9 Educators and Economists

Educational analysts and economists should learn from each other. Economists have traditionally assumed that a student's aptitude as measured by their permanent learning rate was either fixed in the student at birth or determined by cultural background. This assumption has led economists to recommend the allocation of relatively more resources to students with higher "mental capacities." The oversight of the orthodox economic theory of learning is the phenomenon of how an instructional target(V^*) interacts with a pupil's aptitude(V_i) to partially determine a student's learning rate(K_i). This omission has led economists to make faulty policy recommendations. As argued, allocating relatively more resources to higher-aptitude pupils has the damaging effect of exacerbating inequality and decreasing efficiency.

Again, Bloom(1976) and his doctoral candidates at the University of Chicago present a bibliography of educational-psychological work that has conclusions contrary to the learning assumptions made by economists. When summarizing this work, Bloom(1976) describes three eras that educational thought has passed through:

1. (Pre 1960) "There are good learners and there are poor learners."
2. (1960's) "There are faster learners and there are slower learners."
3. (Post 1960's) "Most students become very similar with regard to learning ability, rate of learning, and motivation for further learning - when provided with favorable learning conditions."(i.e. zero instructional error)

The orthodox economic theory of learning remains stuck in either stage one or two. Economists need to accept the results on Mastery Learning and learning capital and thus progress into stage three.

On the other hand, educators have not appreciated the large opportunity costs involved in minimizing instructional error or providing the optimal learning conditions for pupils in a single school characterized by heterogeneous aptitudes. The term 'equality of opportunity' is a misnomer in a school with diverse aptitudes and a pupil-teacher ratio greater than one. Educators prefer to continually increase expenditures per-pupil(e_i) in order to mitigate the effects of high aptitude dispersion. Economists, on the other hand, begin at the opposite end of this relation: σ and $\Delta\sigma$ should be minimized in order to do the best one can with the given level of funding(e_i).

The economists' starting point is superior. Suppose public schools are given more funding. If higher expenditures per-pupil(e_i) are used to offer more aptitude-targeted programs or tracks within the school, then inequality or $\Delta\sigma$ increases(regression 20) which decreases *dynamic efficiency*(regression one) and creates an even larger need for more funding to provide for "equality of opportunity" or equal and high learning rates. Allocating more money to the public schools under these conditions is like giving more addictive drugs to a "junky." The more money and drugs they get, the more they need in order to attain their goals of "becoming equal" or "getting a fix." So ignoring the economic notion of competing ends and scarce resources leads to mistaken utterances like the following:

> The increasing evidence... that investment in the education of humans pays off at a greater rate than does capital investment suggests that we cannot return to an economy of scarcity of educational opportunity(Bloom; 1968, p. 75).

> From the point of view of most professional educators, more resources are by definition highly desirable... . As educational research in the 1970's and early 1980's began to focus on these variables, certain attributes associated with effective public schools were identified. These findings were relatively consistent across diverse contexts and research methods.
> - Anthony S. Bryk, Valerie E. Lee, and Peter B. Holland
>   *Catholic Schools and the Common Good*(1993, p. 56).

> This paper proposes an extension in the scope of educational opportunity... .The curriculum of the American system of education would be differentiated to take account of the wide range in backgrounds, aptitudes, interests, and life goals of a heterogeneous population... . A system of education of such scope and quality for a rising population will cost much more than is presently being expended... . Let us say that it will cost at least twice what it is costing now.
> - Horace Mann Lecture(1964) *"Critical Issues in American Public Education"* by John K Norton(Professor Emeritus; Teachers College, Columbia University) p. 81-82.

A maximum average learning rate is a most noble service the education establishment can offer a community of pupil/families. And most pupil/families are willing to pay the price for this service provided that more funding does in fact lead to a higher mean learning rate(K_i) and thus higher mean achievement growth(q_i). However, this positive, causal relationship between funding and achievement growth has been mistakenly taken for granted. As evident in 187 estimates of the educational production function, this alleged relationship does not exist within public schools(Hanushek; 1986, 1989). The marginal impact of funding has been zero partly because aptitude dispersion has been too high within public schools. The marginal impact of funding is greater in private schools because aptitude dispersion is smaller.

Finally, in the pursuit of educational excellence, analysts from all the social sciences have employed their respective methods for analyzing and evaluating the performance of our schools. The economic method of constrained optimization used to develop the theory of learning capital is believed most helpful. The economic way of thinking is useful because it directs our thoughts toward the crucial question of how to get the most learning from any level of funding(e_i) and time-on-task(T_i); and away from the question of how to maximize funding and pupil effort. Related to this, the economist offers a final insight for the school debate: Provided that a free-enterprise system of education is instituted and pupil/families aspire to knowledge and understanding; then a society's wealth, measured in money and time-on-task, will naturally flow toward the schools offering a maximum average learning rate.

Note

1   With the large gulfs between aptitude tracks within and between schools one would predict that private tutoring firms would flourish in order to minimize instructional error for students or provide for an investment in future learning capital. In support of this prediction, Lieberman(1989) describes how private tutoring firms such as *Sylvan*, *Huntington*, and *American* are presently expanding rapidly by opening franchise operations throughout the U.S. This should be embarassing to public schools. At the end of a school day and on Saturday mornings when students are at the lowest point on their learning curves, they proceed to purchase these expensive learning services while the public school buildings remain vacant.

Bibliography

Aldridge, Bill G. "A Mathematical Model For Mastery Learning," *Journal of Research in Science Teaching,* 1983, 20(1), pp. 1 - 17.

Alexander, K.A. and A.M. Pallas "School Sector and Cognitive Performance: When is a little a little?" *Sociology of Education,* April, 1985, pp. 115 - 127.

Alexander, K.A. and A.M. Pallas "Private Schools and Public Policy: New Evidence on Cognitive Achievement in Public and Private Schools," *Sociology of Education,* 1983, 56, pp. 170 - 182.

Anderson, L.W. *Time and School Learning,* Unpublished Doctoral Dissertation: University of Chicago, 1973.

Arlin, M.N. *Learning Rate and Learning Rate Variance Under Mastery Learning Conditions,* Unpublished Doctoral Dissertation: University of Chicago, 1973.

Arnott, R. and J. Rowse "Peer Group Effects and Educational Attainment," *Journal of Public Economics,* 1987, 32, pp. 287 - 305.

Astin, Alexander W. "Educational 'Choice': Its Appeal May Be Illusory," *Sociology of Education,* October 1992, 65, pp. 255-260.

Averch, H.A., S.J. Carroll, T.S. Donaldson, H.J. Kiesling, and J. Pincus *How Effective is Schooling? A Critical Review and Synthesis of Research Findings,* Educational Technology Publications: Englewood Cliffs, N.J., 1974.

Bartell, Ernest C.S.C. *Costs and Benefits of Catholic Elementary and Secondary Schools,* Notre Dame Press: Notre Dame, Indiana, 1969.

Becker, Gary S. *Treatise on the Human Family,* Harvard University Press, Cambridge, Mass.(enlarged edition, 1991).

Becker, Gary S. *Human Capital,* National Bureau of Economic Research: New York, 2nd ed., 1975.

Becker, Gary S. "A Theory of the Allocation of Time," *Economic Journal,* September 1965, pp. 493 - 517.

Becker, William E. "The Educational Process and Student Achievement Given Uncertainty in Measurement," *American Economic Review,* March 1982, pp. 229 - 236.

Becker, William E. "Economic Education Research: Part II, New Directions in Theoretical Model Building," *Journal of Economic Education,* Spring 1983b, 14, pp. 4 - 10.

Becker, W., W. Greene, and S. Rosen "Research on High School Economic Education," *American Economic Review Proceedings,* May 1990, 80, pp. 14 - 22.

Benson, Charles *The Economics of Public Education,* Houghton Mifflin and Co.: Boston, MA., 2nd ed., 1968.

Benson, Charles, et. al. "State and Local Fiscal Relationships in Public Education in California," *Report of the Senate Fact Finding Committee on Revenue and Taxation*, Senate of the State of California: Sacramento, Ca., 1965.

Blaug, Mark "The Empirical Status of Human Capital Theory: A Slightly Jaundiced Survey," *Journal of Economic Literature*, September 1976, pp. 827 - 856.

Blaug, Mark *Economics of Education: A Selected Annotated Bibliography*, Pergamon Press: New York, New York, 3rd ed., 1978.

Blaug, Mark *The Economics of Education and the Education of an Economist*. New York Press: Washington Square, New York, 1987.

Block, J.H. (Ed.) *Schools, Society, and Mastery Learning*, Holt, Rhinehart and Winston: New York, 1974.

Bloom, Benjamin S. *Stability and Change in Human Characteristics*, John Wiley and Sons, Inc.: New York, 1964.

Bloom, Benjamin S. 1976. *Human Characteristics and School Learning*, McGraw-Hill: New York, 1976.

Bloom, Benjamin S. "Time and School Learning," *American Psychologist,* 1974,29, pp. 682-688.

Bowles, Samuel S. "Towards Equality?" *Harvard Educational Review*, 1968, 38 no. 1, p. 89.

Bowles, Samuel S. "Towards an Educational Production Function," *Education, Income, and Human Capital*, edited by W.L. Hansen, Columbia University Press: New York, 1970.

Bowles, Samuel and Herbert Gintis *Schooling in Capitalist America: Educational Reform and the Contradictions of Economic Life*, Basic Books: New York, 1976.

Bowles, Samuel and Herbert Gintis "Schooling in Capitalist America: A Reply to Our Critics," *Bowles and Gintis Revisited,* edited by Mike Cole, Falmer Press: London, 1988.

Bowles, Samuel S. and Henry M. Levin "The Determinants of Scholastic Achievement - An Appraisal of Some Recent Evidence," *Journal of Human Resources*, 3, 1968, pp. 393-400.

Brown, B.W., and D. H. Saks "The Production and Distribution of Cognitive Skills Within Schools," *Journal of Political Economy*, 1975, 83(3), pp. 571 - 593.

Bryk, Anthony S., Valerie E. Lee, and Peter B. Holland *Catholic Schools and the Common Good*, Harvard University Press, Cambridge, Mass., 1993.

Buetow, Harold A. *The Catholic School: Its Roots, Identity, and Future*, Crossroad Publishing: New York, New York, 1988.

Burkhead, J., T.G. Fox, and J. W. Holland, *Input and Output in Large-City High Schools*, Syracuse University Press: Syracuse, New York, 1967.

Butler, R.J. and D.H. Monk "The Cost of Public Schooling in New York State: The Role of Scale and Efficiency in 1978-1979," *Journal of Human Resources*, Summer 1985, 20, pp. 361 - 381.

Cain, G.G.; and A.S. Goldberger "Public and Private Schools Revisited," *Sociology of Education*, 1983, 56, pp. 208 - 218.

Carnoy, Martin and Henry M. Levin *The Limits of Educational Reform*, David Mckay: New York, 1976.

Carroll, S.J., and R.E. Park *The Search For Equity in School Finance*. Ballinger Publishing Co.: Cambridge, Mass., 1983.

Carroll, John B. "A Model for School Learning," *Teachers College Record*, 1963, 64, pp. 723 - 733.

Carroll, John B. "The 'Model of School Learning': Progress of an Idea," in *Perspectives on Instructional Time*, Fisher, C. and D.C. Berliner(eds.), Longman: New York,1985.

Carroll, John B. "The Carroll Model: A 25-year Retrospective and Prospective View," *Educational Researcher,* January-February 1989, pp. 26 - 31.

Chizmar, John F. and Thomas A. Zak "Modeling Multiple Outputs in Educational Production Functions," *American Economic Review*, May 1983, 73(2), pp. 18-22.

Chubb, J.E. and T.M. Moe *Politics, Markets, and America's Schools,* The Brookings Institution: Washington, D.C., 1990.

Cohn, Elchanan "Economies of Scale in Iowa High School Operations," *Journal of Human Resources*, Fall 1968, 3(4), pp. 422 - 434.

Cohn, Elchanan *The Economics of Education*, Ballinger Publishing: Cambridge, MA., 1979.

Cohn, E. and S.D. Millman *Input -Output Analysis in Public Education*, Ballinger Publishing Company: Cambridge, MA., 1975.

Coleman, James S. "The Concept of Equality of Opportunity," *Harvard Educational Review*, 1968, 38(1), p. 7.

Coleman, James S. "Families and Schools," *Educational Researcher,* August-September 1987, 16(6), pp. 32 -38.

Coleman, James S. "Some Points on Choice in Education," *Sociology of Education*, October 1992, 65(4), pp. 260-262.

Coleman, J.S., E.Q. Cambell, C.F. Hobson, J. McPartland, A.M. Mood, F.D. Weinfeld, F.D., and R.L. York *Equality of Educational Opportunity*, U.S. Department of Health, Education, and Welfare; Office of Education: U.S. Government Printing Office, Washington, D.C., 1966.

Coleman, J.S. and T. Hoffer "Response to Tauber-James, Cain-Goldberger, and Morgan," *Sociology of Education,* October 1983, pp. 219 - 234.

Coleman, J.S., T. Hoffer, and A.M. Greeley "Achievement Growth in Public and Catholic Schools," *Sociology of Education,* April 1985, pp. 74 - 97.

Coleman, J.S., T. Hoffer, and S. Kilgore *Public and Private High Schools*, National Center for Education Statistics: Washington, D.C., 1981.

Coleman, J.S., T. Hoffer, and S. Kilgore *High School Achievement*, Basic Books: New York, 1982.

Coleman, J.S., T. Hoffer and S. Kilgore "Questions and Answers: Our Response," *Harvard Educational Review.*, 1981, 51, pp. 526 - 545.

Coons, John E. and Stephen D. Sugarman *Education By Choice: The Case for Familiy Control*, University of California Press, 1978.

Cremin, Lawrence A.(ed.) *The Republic and The School: Horace Mann on the Education of Free Men*, Bureau of Publications: Teachers College; Columbia University, New York, 1957.

Cremin, Lawrence A. *Popular Education and its Discontents*(1990), Harper & Row, New York.

Cronbach, L.J., and R. E. Snow *Aptitudes and Instructional Methods: A Handbook for Research on Interactions*, Irvington Publishers: New York, 1977.

Davisson, W.I. and F.J. Bonello *Computer Assisted Instruction in Economic Education: A Case Study*, Notre Dame Press: Notre Dame, Indiana; 1976.

Dewey, John *Democracy and Education*, The Free Press: New York, 1966.

Finn, Chester E. Jr. *We Must Take Charge: Our Schools and our Future*, The Free Press: New York, New York; 1991.

Flannery, Austin(ed.) *Vatican Council II: The Conciliar and Post Conciliar Documents*, 2 vols., Costello: Northport, N.Y., 1982.

Fisher, C.W. and D.C. Berliner *Perspectives on Instructional Time*, Longman: New York, 1985.

Friedman, Milton "The Role of Government in Education" in *Capitalism and Freedom*; University of Chicago Press: Chicago, Ill., 1962, pp. 85 - 107.

Froomkin, J.T., D.T. Jamison, and R. Radner *Education as an Industry*, Ballinger Publishing Co.: National Bureau of Economic Research, 1976.

Garner, W.T. "The Public Economics of Mastery Learning," *Educational Technology,* 1978, 18, pp. 12 - 17.

Glasman, Naftaly S. and Israel Biniaminov "Input-Output Analysis in Schools," *Review of Educational Research*, Winter 1981, 51(4), pp. 509-39.

Goldberg, M., A.H. Passow, and J. Justman, *The Effects of Ability Grouping*, Teachers College Press: New York, 1966.

Goldberger, Arthur S. and Cain, Glen G. "The Causal Analysis of Cognitive Outcomes in the Coleman, Hoffer, and Kilgore Report," *Sociology of Education*, April/July 1982, 55, pp. 103 - 122.

Greeley, A.M. *Catholic High Schools and Minority Students*, Transaction Books: New Brunswick, N.J.; 1982.

Gurwitz, A.S. *The Economics of Public School Finance*, Ballinger Publishing Co.: Cambridge, Ma.; 1982.

Gyimah-Brempong, Kwabena and Anthony O. Gyapong "Production of Education: Are Socioeconomic Characteristics Important Factors?" *Eastern Economic Journal*, October-December 1991, XVII(4).

Hallinan, Maureen T. "Tracking: From Theory to Practice" *Sociology of Education*, April 1994, vol. 67 no. 2, pp. 79 - 84.

Hamilton, B. W. "Capitalization of Intrajurisdictional Differences in Local Tax Prices," *American Economic Review*, December 1976, 66(5), pp. 743 - 753.

Hansen, W.L., A.C. Kelley, and B.A. Weisbrod "Economic Efficiency and the Distribution of Benefits from College Instruction," *American Economic Review*, May 1970, 60.

Hanushek, Eric A. *Education and Race: An Analysis of the Educational Production Process*, Lexington Books: Lexington, Mass., 1972.

Hanushek, Eric A. "The Economics of Schooling: Production and Efficiency in Public Schools," *Journal of Economic Literature*, 1986, 24(3), pp. 1141 - 1177.

Hanushek, Eric A. "The Impact of Differential Expenditures on School Performance," *Educational Researcher,* May 1989, pp. 45 - 51.

Hanushek, Eric A. (editor) *Making Schools Work: Improving Performance and Controlling Costs*, The Brookings Institution (Washington, D.C., 1994)

Henderson, V., P. Miezkowski, and Y. Sauvageau "Peer Group Effects and Educational Production Functions," *Journal of Public Economics,* 1978, 10, pp. 97 - 106.

Heynemen, Stephen P. and William Loxley "The Effect of Primary-School Quality on Academic Achievement Across Twenty-nine High and Low Income Countries," *American Journal of Sociology*, May 1983, 88, pp. 1162-94.

Heyns, B. and T.L. Hilton "The Cognitive Tests for High School and Beyond: An Assessment," *Sociology of Education,* 1982, 55, pp. 89 - 102.

Hirschman, A.E. *Exit, Voice, and Loyalty*; Harvard University Press: Cambridge, MA., 1970.

Hume, David "Of the Original Contract," in *Essays, Moral and Political*; 1748, p. 291.

James, T. and H.M. Levin(eds.) *Public Dollars for Private Schools: The Case of Tuition Tax Credits*, Temple University Press: Philadelphia, Pa., 1983.

Jencks, C. "How Much Do High School Students Learn?" *Sociology of Education,* April 1985, pp. 128 - 135.

Jencks, C.S., M. Smith, H. Acland, M.J. Bane, D.K. Cohen, H. Gintis, B. Heyns, and S. Michelson *Inequality: A Reassessment of the Effect of Family and Schooling in America*, Basic Books: New York, 1972.

Jensen, G.F. "Explaining Differences in Academic Behavior Between Public-School and Catholic-School Students," *Sociology of Education*, January 1986, pp. 32 - 41.

John Paul II "On the Hundredth Anniversary of Rerum Novarum," *Centesimus Annus,* United States Catholic Conference: Washington D.C., 1991, Publication No. 436-8.

John Paul II "Catechesis in Our Time(Catechesi tradendae)," #72, in Austin Flannery(ed.) *Vatican Council II: The Conciliar and Post Conciliar Documents*, 2 vols., Costello: Northport, N.Y., 1982.

Jones, C. M., Clarke, G. Mooney, H. McWilliams, I. Crawford, B. Stephenson, and R. Tourangeau *High School and Beyond 1980 Sophomore Cohort First Follow Up (1982) Data File User's Manual*, National Center for Education Statistics: Washington D.C.

Katz, Michael B. *The Irony of School Reform*, Harvard University Press: Cambridge, 1968.

Katzman, M.T. *The Political Economy of Urban Schools*, Harvard University Press: Cambridge, Ma., 1971.

Kelley, A.C. "The Student as a Utility Maximizer," *Journal of Economic Education*, Spring 1975, 6, pp. 82 - 92.

Kiesling, H.J. *The Study of Cost and Quality of New York School Districts: Final Report*, U.S. Department of Health, Education, and Welfare, Office of Education: Washington, D.C., 1970.

Kilgore, S. "Statistical Evidence, Selectivity Effects and Program Placement: Response to Alexander and Pallas," *Sociology of Education,* 1983, 56, pp. 182 - 186.

Layard, Richard and George Psacharopoulos "The Screening Hypothesis and the Returns to Education," *Journal of Political Economy*, 1974, 82(5).

Lee, Valerie E. and Anthony S. Bryk "A Multilevel Model of the Social Distribution of High School Acheivement," *Sociology of Education*, 1989, vol. 62(July) pp. 172-192.

Lee, V.E., R.F. Dedrick, and J.B. Smith "The Effect Of The Social Organization of Schools on Teachers' Efficacy and Satisfaction," *Sociology of Education*, July 1991, 64(3), pp. 190 - 208.

Levin, H. "Economic Efficiency and Educational Production," in Froomkin, J.T., D.T. Jamison, and R. Radner *Education as an Industry*, Ballinger Publishing Co.: National Bureau of Economic Research, 1976.

Levin, H. "Mapping the Economics of Education: An Introductory Essay," *Educational Researcher*, May 1989, pp. 13 - 16.

Levin, H. "The Economics of Educational Choice," *Economics of Education Review*, vol. 10, no. 2, pp. 137-158.

Levin, T. *The Effect of Content Prerequisite and Process-oriented Experiences on Application Ability in the Learning of Probability*, Unpublished doctoral dissertation, University of Chigago: Chicago, Ill., 1975.

Lieberman, M. *Privatization and Educational Choice*, St. Martin's Press: New York, New York, 1989.

Lieberman, M. *Public Education: An Autopsy*, Harvard University Press, Cambridge, Mass.; 1993.

Lillydahl, Jane "Academic Achievement and Part-time Employment of High School Students," *Journal of Economic Education,* Summer 1990.

Linder, S.B. *The Harried Leisure Class*, Columbia University Press, New York, 1970.

Lipset, Seymor Martin "Equal or Better in America," *Columbia University Forum,* Spring 1961, p. 17.

Lopez, Jane S. "Do Additional Expenditures Increase Achievement in the High School Economics Class?" *Journal of Economic Education,* Summer 1990, pp. 277 - 286.

Mehan, Hugh "Understanding Inequality in Schools: The Contribution of Interpretive Studies," in *Sociology of Education,* January 1992, 65, pp. 1-20.

McClusky, N. ed.(1964) *Catholic Education in America: A Documentary History.* Teachers' College, Columbia University; New York.

McKenzie, R.B. "Where is the Economics in Economic Education?" *Journal of Economic Education,* Fall 1977.

McKenzie, R.B. and R.J. Staaf (1974) *An Economic Theory of Learning: Student Sovereignty and Academic Freedom,* University Press: Blacksburg, Va., 1974.

Mill, John S. *On Liberty*(1859), The MacMillan Company; New York, 1926.

Miller, George A. "The Challenge of Universal Literacy," *Science,* September 1988, 241, pp. 1293 - 1299.

Mills, Edwin S. and Bruce W. Hamilton *Urban Economics,* Scott, Foresman and Company; Glenview, Illinois and London; 1984, 3rd edition.

Mincer, J. "Investment in Human Capital and Personal Income Distribution," *Journal of Political Economy*, August 1958, 66, pp. 281 - 302.

Mollenkopf, Wm. G., and S.D. Melville, S.D. *A Study of Secondary School Characteristics as Related to Test Scores,* Educational Testing Service: Princeton, Research Bulletin RB-56-6, 1956.

Murnane, R.J. *The Impact of School Resources on the Learning of Inner City Children,* Ballinger Publishing Co.: Cambridge, Mass., 1975.

Murnane, R.J. "The Uncertain Consequences of Tuition Tax Credits: An Analysis of Student Achievement and Economic Incentives," in James, T. and H.M. Levin(eds.) *Public Dollars for Private Schools: The Case of Tuition Tax Credits*, Temple University Press: Philadelphia, Pa., 1883.

Murnane, R.J. "A Review Essay - Comparisons of Public and Private Schools: Lessons From the Uproar," *The Journal of Human Resources*, Spring 1984, XIX(2).

Murnane, R. J., Rebecca A. Maynard, and James C. Ohls "Home Resources and Children's Achievement," *Review of Economics and Statistics*, August 1981, 63(3), pp. 369-77.

Murphy, Joseph (ed.) *The Educational Reform Movement of the 1980's: Perspectives and Cases*, McCutchan Publishing Corporation: Berkeley, California, 1990.

Musgrave, Richard A. *Public Finance in Theory and Practice*, McGraw-Hill Book Co.: New York, 1989.

National Commission on Excellence in Education *A Nation at Risk: The Imperative For Educational Reform*, Government Printing Office: Washington D.C.(Stock no. 065-000-00177-2), April 1983.

National Conference of Catholic Bishops *Economic Justice For All: Pastoral Letter on Catholic Social Teaching and The U.S. Economy*, United States Catholic Conference, Inc.: Washington D.C.

National Education Association *Ability Grouping*, NEA Research Division: Washington, D.C.(Research Summary, 53), 1968.

New York State Department of Education *Performance Indicators in Education, Local District Results*, Bureau of School Program Evaluation: Albany; 1972, 1974, 1975.

Noell, Jay "Public and Catholic Schools: A Reanalysis of Public and Private Schools," *Sociology of Education*, April-July 1982, 55, pp. 123 - 132.

Norton, John K. *Critical Issues in American Public Education*, Horace Mann Lecture-1964, University of Pittsburgh Press, 1965.

Oates, Wallace E. "The Effects of Property Taxes and Local Spending on Property Values: An Empirical Study of Tax Capitalization and the Tiebout Hypothesis," *Journal of Political Economy*, November/December 1969, 77, pp. 957 - 971.

O'Connor, Edward D. C.S.C. *The Catholic Vision*, Our Sunday Visitor, Inc., 1992.

Olson, M. Jr. *The Logic of Collective Action*, Harvard University Press: Cambridge, MA., 1965.

Ozcelik, D.A. *Student Involvement in the Learning Process*, Unpublished doctoral dissertation, University of Chicago: Chicago, Ill., 1974.

Paine, Thomas *The Rights of Man*(1792), E.P. Dutton and Co. Inc.: New York, 1935.

Psacharopoulos, George(ed.) *Economics of Education: Research and Studies*, Pergamon Press: Oxford; New York, 1987.

Perl, L.J. "Family Background, Secondary School Expenditure, and Student Ability," *Journal of Human Resources,* 1973, 8(2), pp. 156 - 180.

Pius XI "The Christian Education of Youth," in *Five Great Encyclicals*, Paulist: New York, 1939, p. 54.

Purkey, Stewart C. and M.S. Smith "Effective Schools: A Review," *The Elementary School Journal,* 1983, 83(4), pp. 427 - 451.

Prince, Kipps, Wilhelm, and Wetzel "Scholastic Effort: An Empirical Test of Student Choice Models," *Journal of Economic Education,* Summer 1981.

Rawls, John *A Theory of Justice,* Harvard University Press: Cambridge, Massachusetts, 1971.

Riew, John "Economies of Scale in High School Operations," *Review of Economics and Statistics,* 1966, 48, pp. 280 - 287.

Roemer, John E. "Providing Equal Educational Opportunity: Public Vs. Voucher Schools," *Social Philosophy and Policy,* 1992, 9(1), pp. 291 - 309.

Rosenbaum, James E. *Making Inequality: the hidden curriculum of high school tracking,* Wiley: New York, 1976.

Rosenbaum, P. and D. Rubin "The Central Role of the Propensity Score in Observational Studies for Causal Effects," *Biometrika,* 1983, 70. pp. 41 - 55.

Rudy, Willis *Schools in an Age of Mass Culture: An Exploration of Selected Themes in the History of Twentieth-Century American Education,* Prentice-Hall, Inc.; Englewood Cliffs, N.J., 1965.

Sandler, Todd and John T. Tschirhart "The Economic Theory of Clubs: An Evlauative Survey," *Journal of Economic Literature,* December 1980, 18(4), pp. 1481 - 1521.

Schmidt, Robert M. "Who Maximizes What?: A Study in Student Time Allocation," *American Economics Association Papers and Proceedings;* May 1983, pp. 23 - 28.

Schultz, T.W. "Investment in Human Capital," *American Economic Review,* March 1961, pp. 1 - 17.

Schultz, T.W. *The Economic Value of Education,* Columbia University Press: New York, 1963.

Sebold, Frederick D. and Dato, William "School Funding and Student Achievement: An Empirical Analysis," *Public Finance Quarterly,* January 1981, 9(1), p. 91-105.

Smith, M.S. "Equality of Educational Opportunity: The Basic Finding Reconsidered," In *On Equality of Educational Opportunity,* edited by F. Mosteller and D.P. Moynihan. New York: Vintage Books, 1972.

Smith, Adam *An Inquiry into the Nature and Causes of the Wealth of Nations*(1776), 2 vols. ed. by Edwin Cannan; Modern Library, New York; 1937.

Spence, A.M. "Job Market Signalling," *Quarterly Journal of Economics,* August 1973, 87, pp. 355-379.

Stiglitz, J. *Economics,* W.W. Norton & Company, Inc.: New York, 1993.

Stiglitz, J. "The Theory of 'Screening,' Education, and the Distribution of Income," *American Economic Review,* June 1975, 65, pp. 283 - 300.

Stiglitz, J. "The Causes and Consequences of the Dependence of Quality on Price," *Journal of Economic Literature*, March 1987, XXV, pp. 1 - 48.

Summers, A.A., and B. L. Wolfe "Do Schools Make a Difference?" *American Economic Review*, 1977, 67, pp. 639 - 652.

Swartz, T.R., W.I. Davisson; and F.J. Bonello "Why Have We Ignored 'The Distribution of Benefits from College Instruction'?" *Journal of Economic Education*, Spring 1980, pp. 28 - 36.

Tawney, R.H. *Equality*, Capricorn Books edition: New York, 1961.

Thorndike, R.M., G.K. Cunningham, R.L. Thorndike, and E.P. Hagen *Measurement and Evaluation in Psychology and Education*, Macmillan Publishing Co.: New York, New York, 5th ed., 1991.

Tiebout, Charles M. "A Pure Theory of Local Expenditures," *Journal of Political Economy*, October 1956, 64, pp. 416 - 424.

Trese, J. Leo *The Faith Explained*, Fides/Claretian; Notre Dame, Indiana, 1965.

United States Department of Education; Office of Educational Research and Improvement *National Excellence: A Case for Developing America's Talent*, U.S. Government Printing Office(October, 1993).

Vernon, P.E. "Heredity-Environment Intelligence Determinants," in *Economics of Education: Research and Studies* , George Psacharopoulos(ed.), Pergamon Press: Oxford; New York, 1987.

Wetzel, J. "Measuring Student Scholastic Effort: An Economic Theory of Learning Approach," *Journal of Economic Education*, Spring 1976, 7(2), pp. 81 - 91.

Wilber, C. and R. Harrison "The Methodological Basis of Institutional Economics: Pattern Model, Storytelling and Holism," *Journal of Economic Issues* 12(1978) pp. 61-89.

Willms, J.D. *Achievement Outcomes in Public and Private Schools: A Closer Look at the 'High School and Beyond' Data*, Stanford Institute for Research on Educational Finance and Governance.

Willms, J.D. "Catholic-school Effects on Academic Achievement: New Evidence from the High School and Beyond Follow-up Study," *Sociology of Education*, 1985, 58, pp. 98 - 114.

Winkler, D.R. "Educational Achievement and School Peer Group Composition," *Journal of Human Resources*, 1975, 10, pp. 189 - 205.

Wolpin, Kenneth I. "Education and Screening," in *American Economic Review*, December 1977, pgs. 949 - 958.

Yeager, Robert J., Peter L. Benson, Michael Guerra, and Bruno V. Manno *The Catholic High School: A National Portrait*, National Catholic Educational Association: Washington D.C., 1985.

Index

Page references followed by *t, f,* or *n* indicate tables, figures, or notes, respectively.

for testing, 79, 84; regression results, 98, 100*t*, 101-2, 105, 112; school comparisons, 34-35, 35*n*; selection homogeneity and, 108, 108*f*, 109*t*; social diversity and, 156; tracking and, 67; voice or exit and, 159. *see also* c-efficiency; dynamic efficiency; selection efficiency

empirical test, 77-123; bias toward null hypotheses, 95-97; data set, 78-79; data weakness, 92-94; equality of opportunity, 97; regression model, 79-92, 80*t*-83*t*; regression results, 98-112, 99*t*-100*t*; statistical vs policy significance, 113

English: tracking in, 135, 157

enrollment: effects on efficiency, 64; public vs private schools, 73

equality: separateness and, 73; voice or exit and, 159

equality of achievement, 17-20; benefits of competition for, 171-73; vouchers and, 172-73

Equality of Educational Opportunity, 7

equality of learning rate, 24, 61

equality of opportunity, 140, 176; and efficiency, 24; gains for public schools, 113, 114*t*; gains with private sector adjusted mean values for σ and Δσ, 137, 138*t*; gains with private sector median values for σ and Δσ, 118, 119*t*; goal of, 61-62; in public vs private schools, 97; regression results, 112

equality of outcomes: and efficiency, 24, 150, 156

equality of students, 24

error. *see* instructional error

ethnic diversity, 72. *see also* diversity

excellence, 143-53; determinants for, 155-63; propositions, 156-57

expected instructional error (μ), 65

expenditures, 176-77; administrative, 122*n*; diminishing returns, 106*f*, 106-7; high school vs district, 92-93; impact on cognitive growth, 167-68; mean values, 95, 96*t*; parameter coefficients for public schools, 7, 8*t*; regression results, 102, 103*t*-104*t*

families: impact on students, 155-56; learning capital and expenditures, 51-52; parental behavior, 66; school characteristics that attract, 59-60

family variables, 81*t*, 85-86; mean values, 95, 96*t*; regression results, 98, 99*t*

friends: possibility of losing, 147

funding, 176-77; budget recommendations, 26; diminishing returns, 106*f*, 106-7; intra-school, 160-61; marginal impact of, 58-59; marginal product of, 122*n*; output per-dollar spent, 51-52; tracking and, 50, 54*n*; voice mechanism for changing allocations, 54*n*. *see also* costs; expenditures

gifted and talented programs, 160